DISC GOLF STAMP

COLORING BOOK

A DISC GOLF COLORING BOOK WITH
RELAXING AND STRESS RELIEVING DESIGNS

TRUE NORTH OF NORMAL

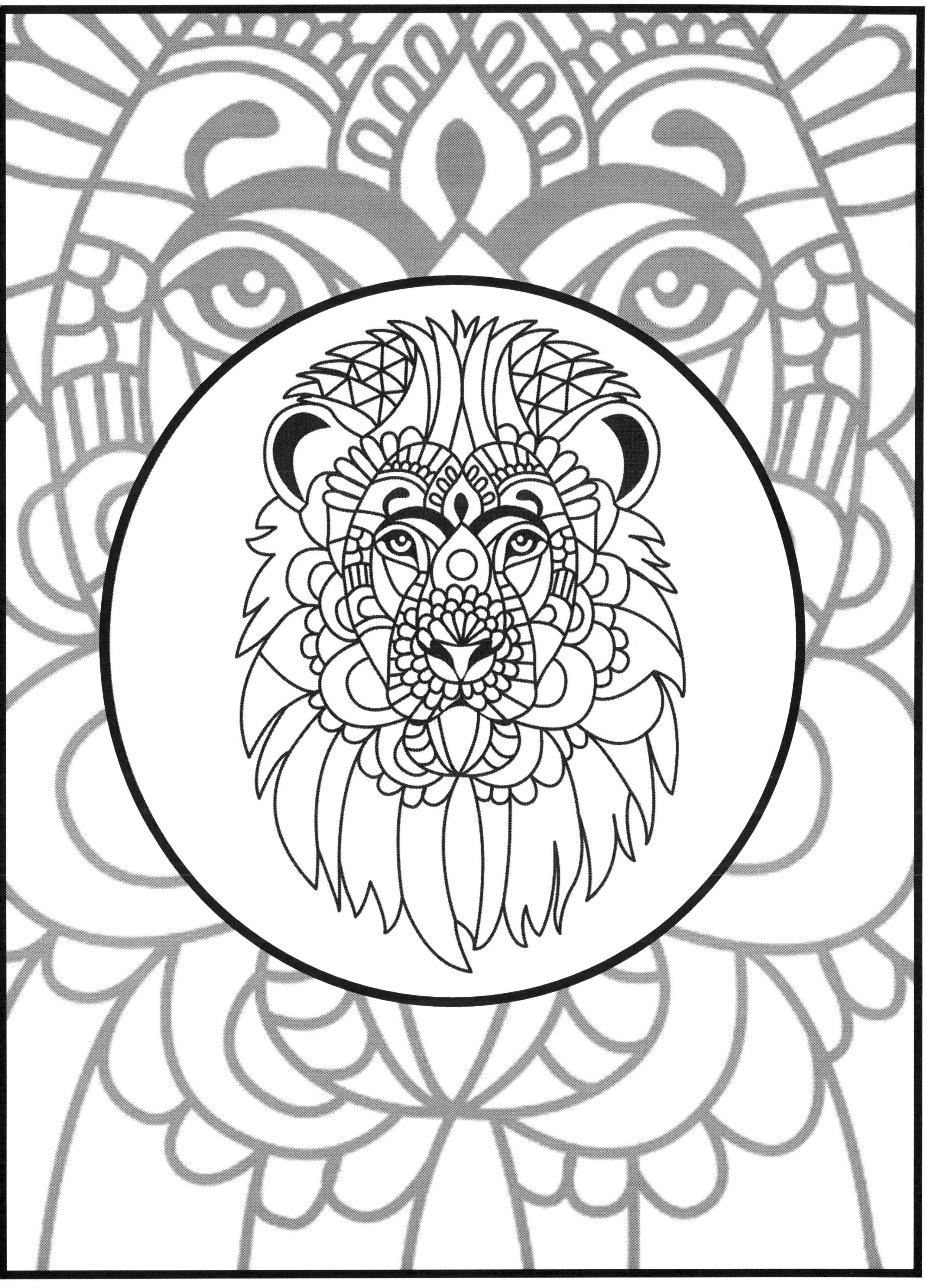

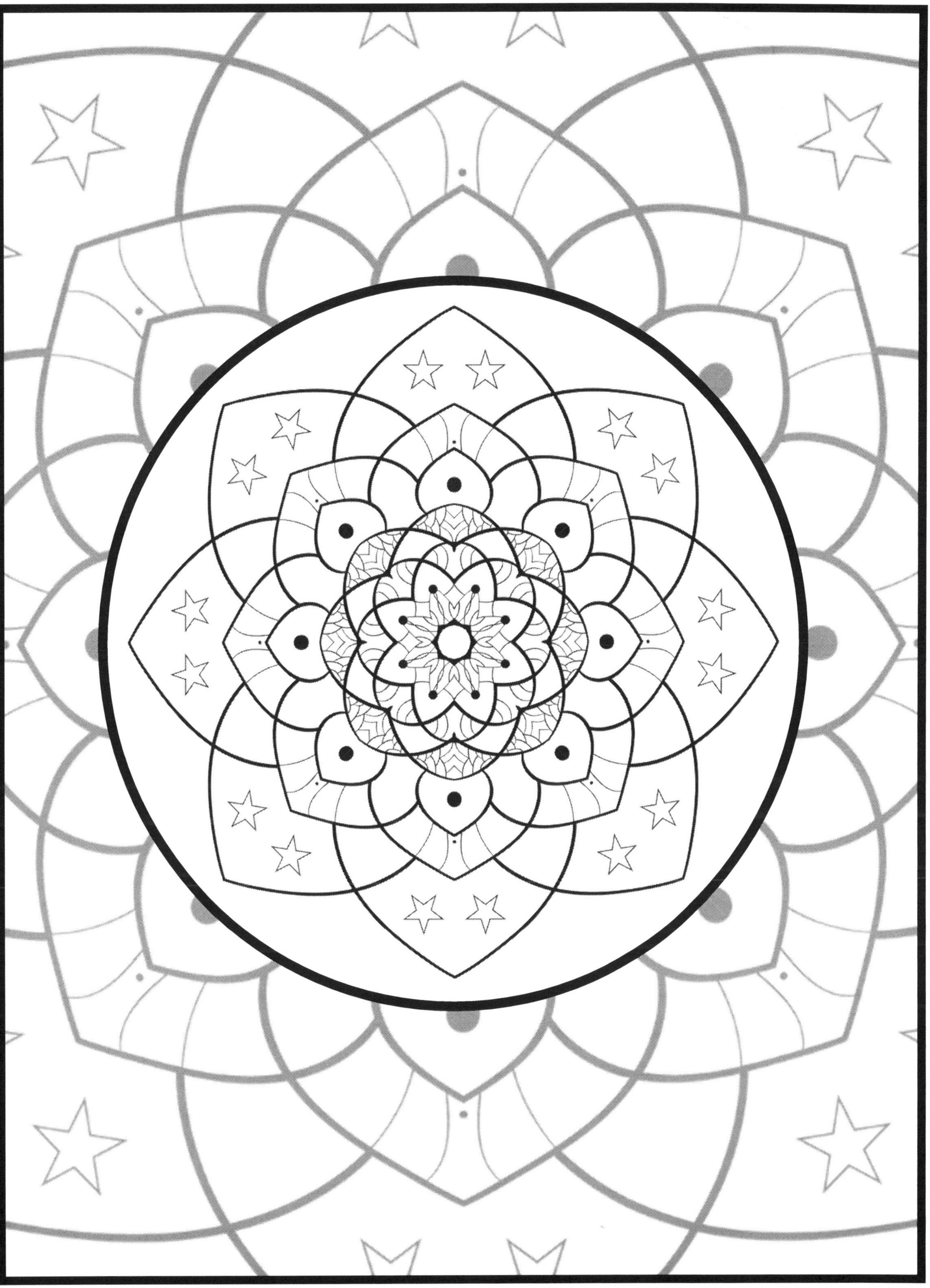

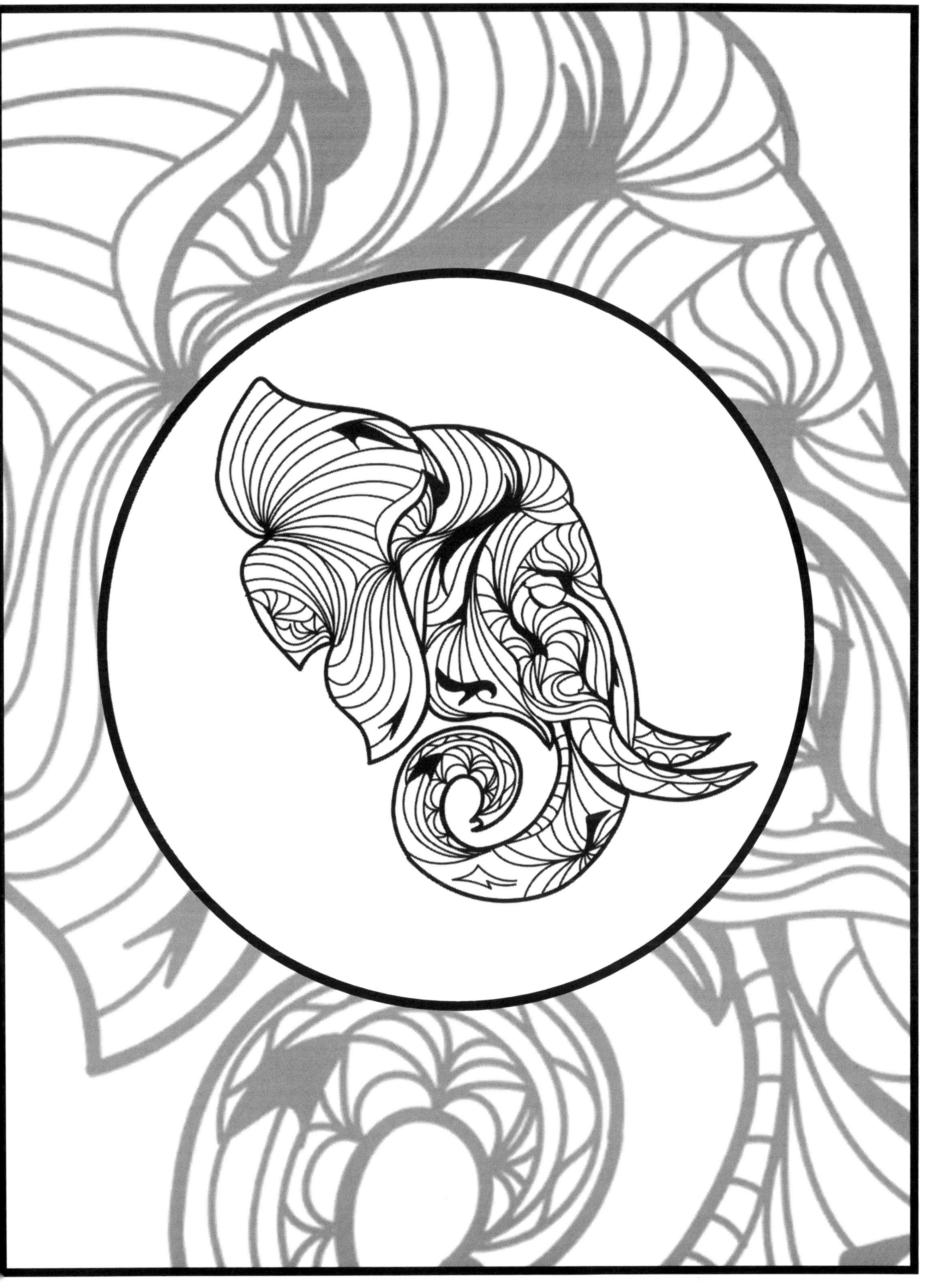

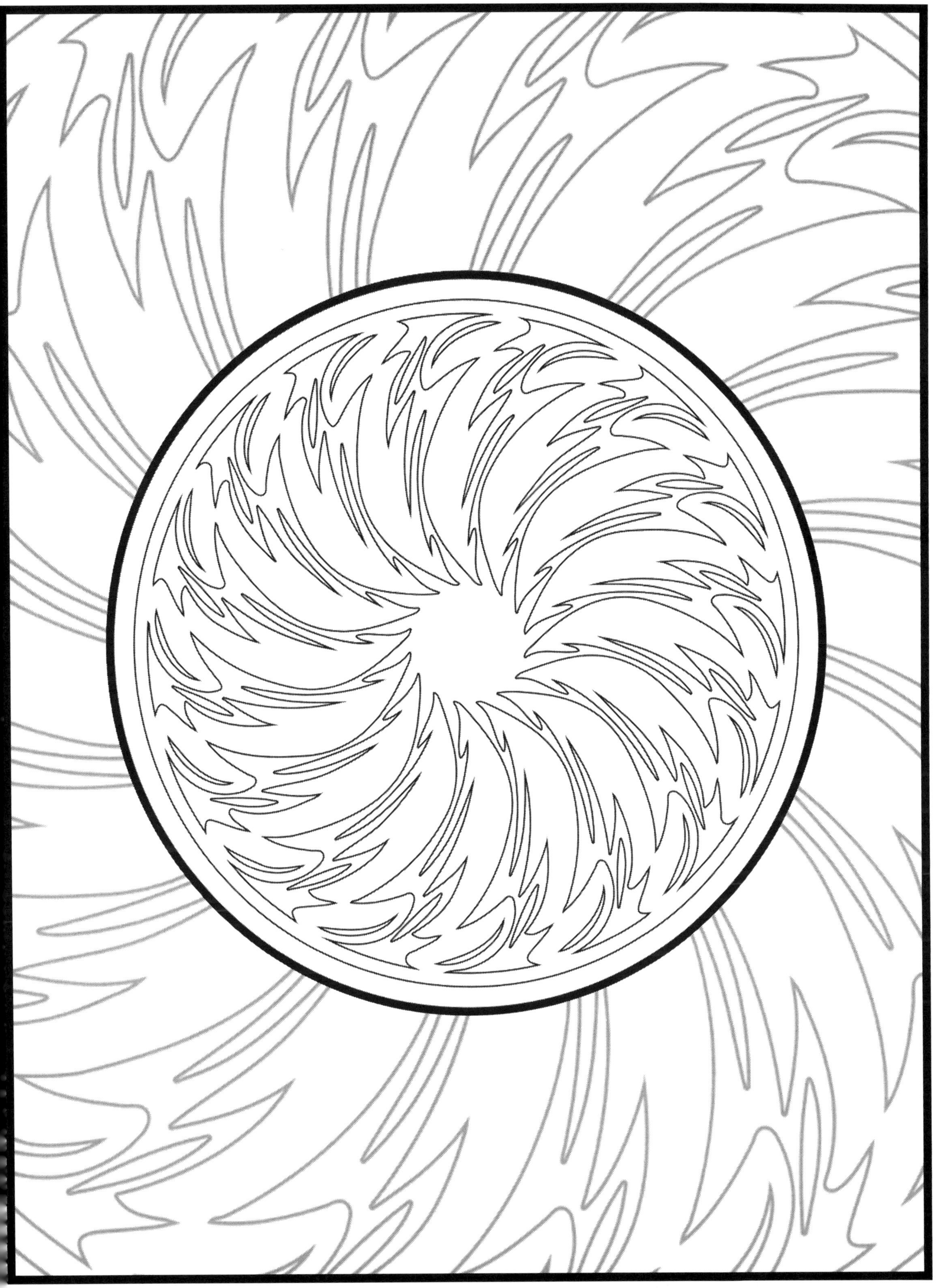

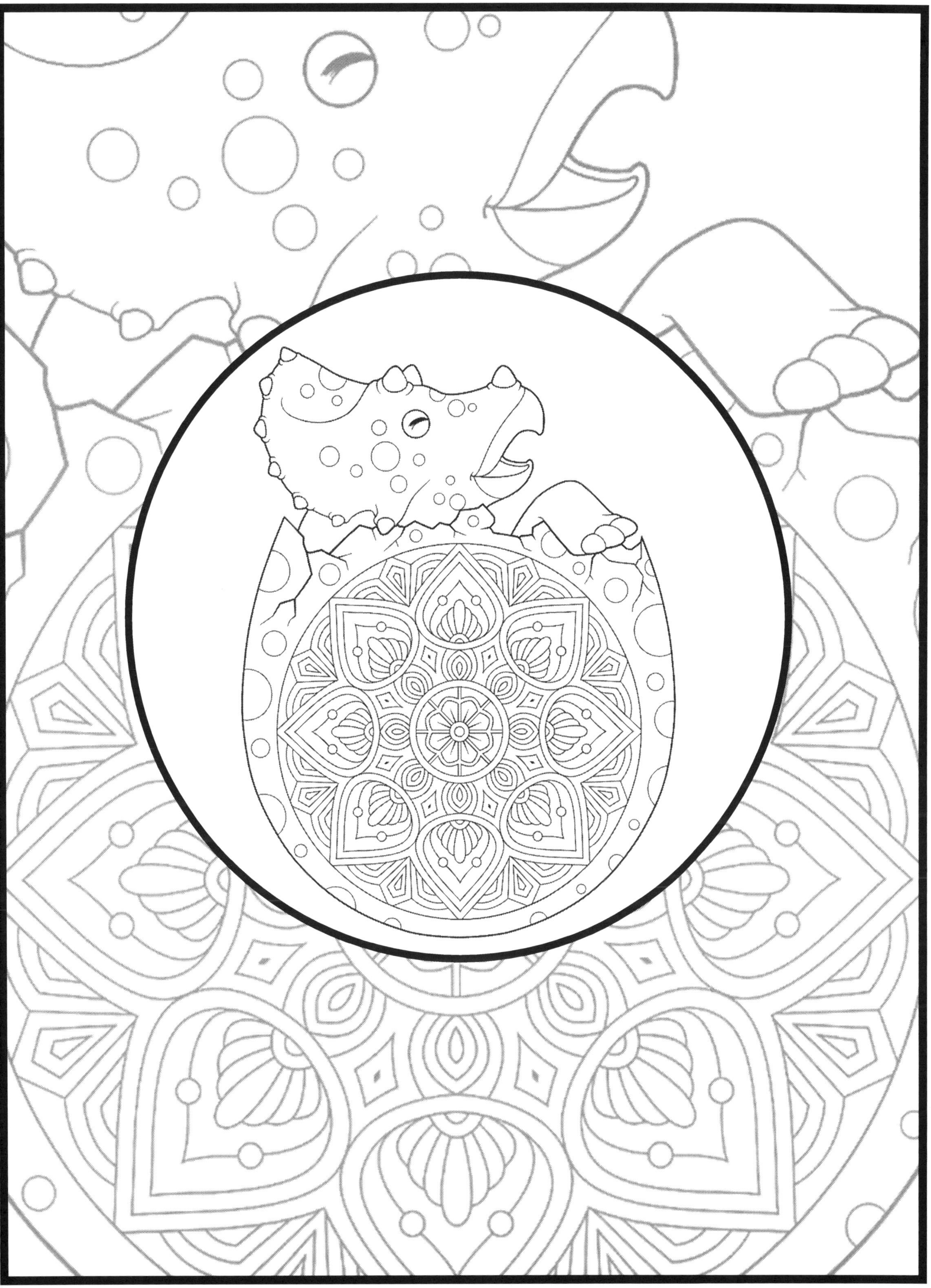

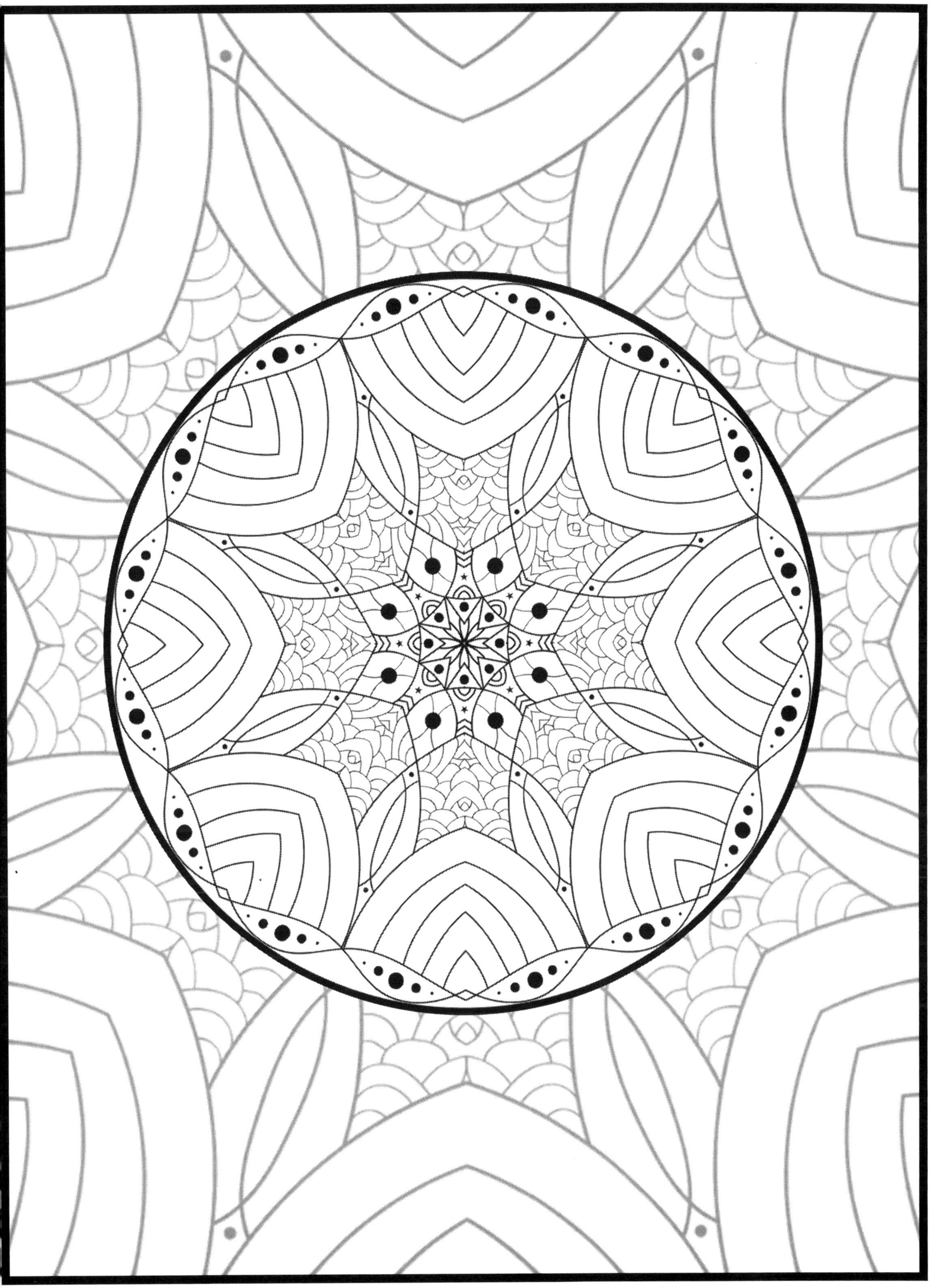

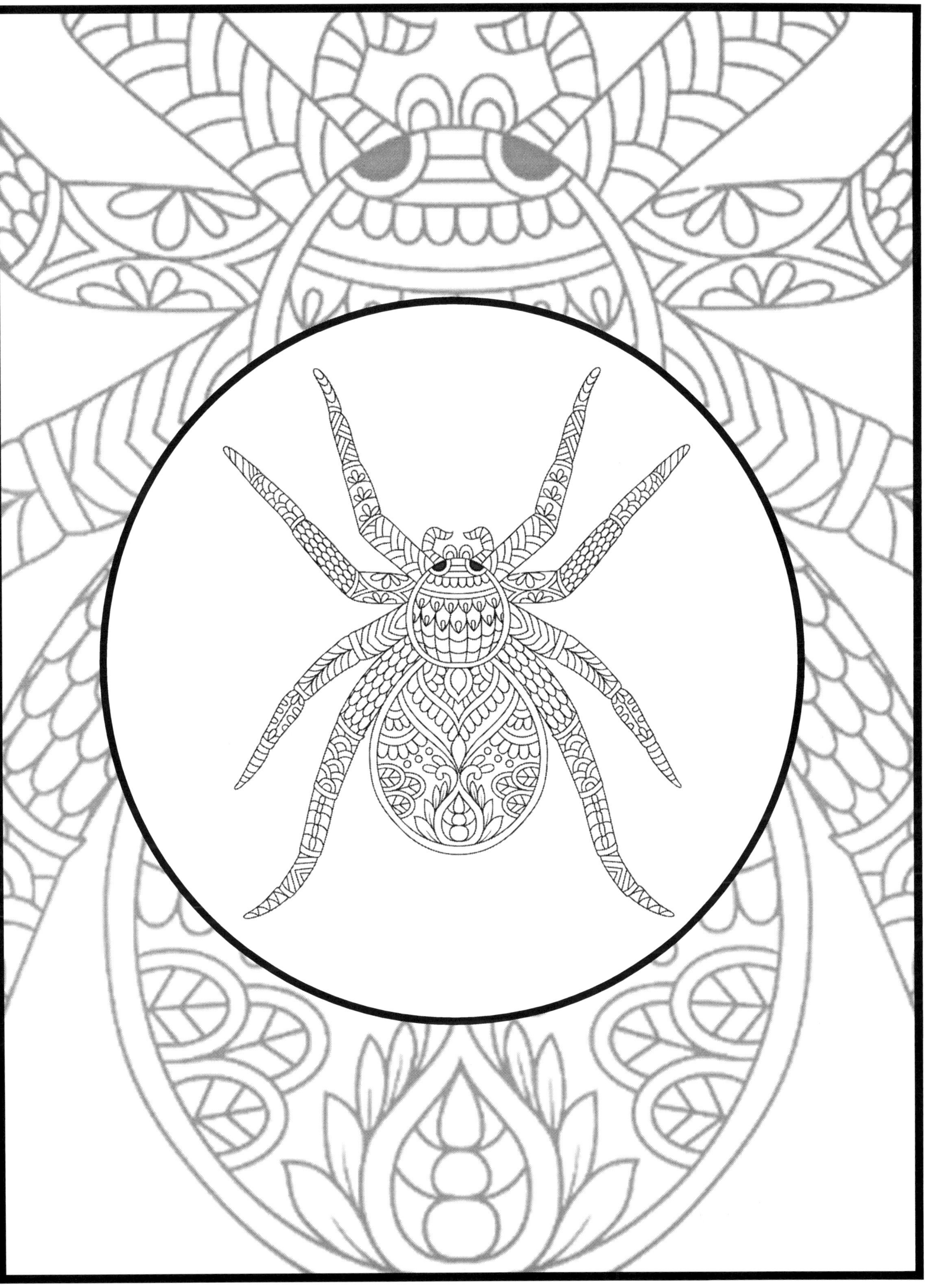

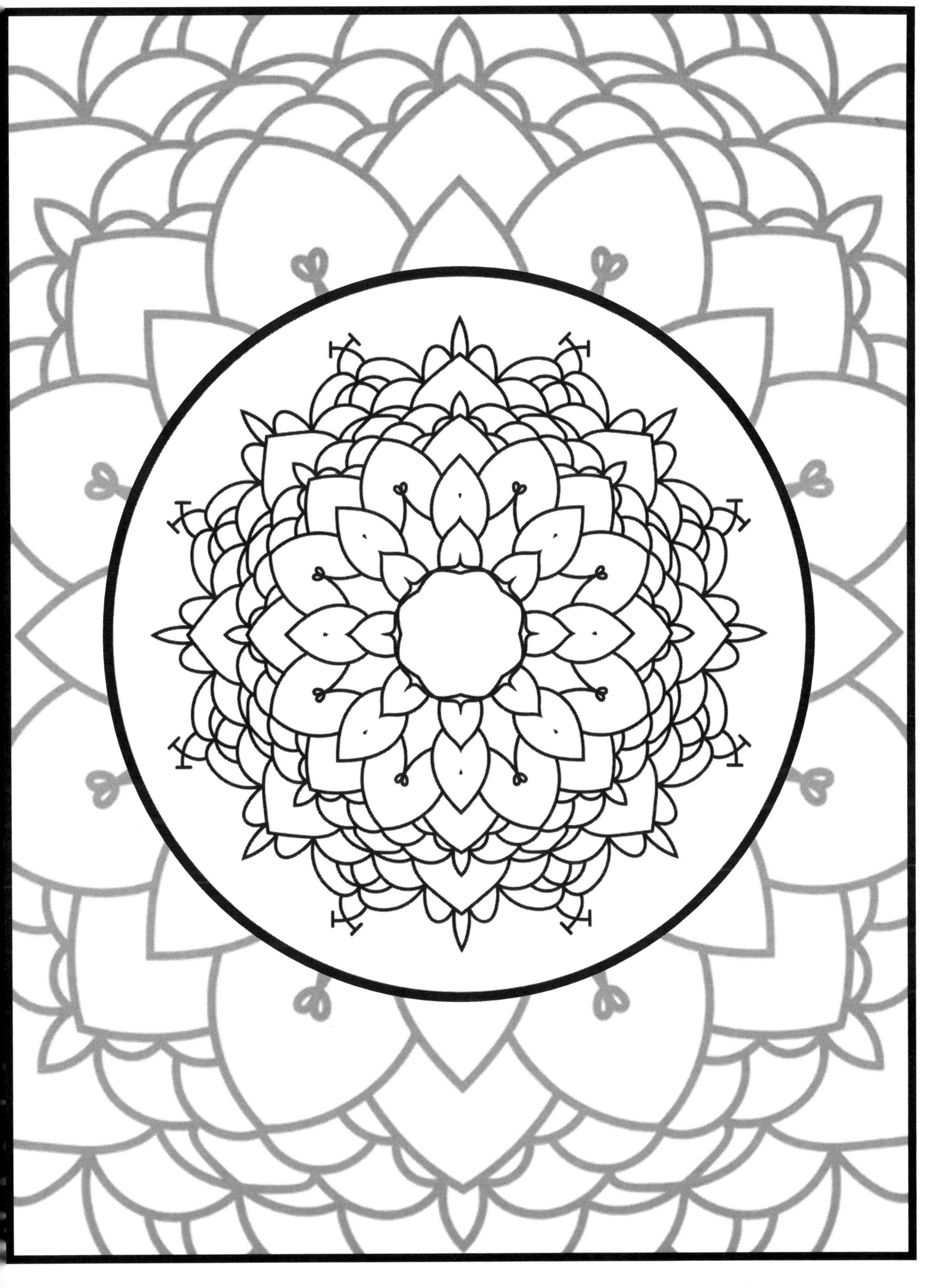

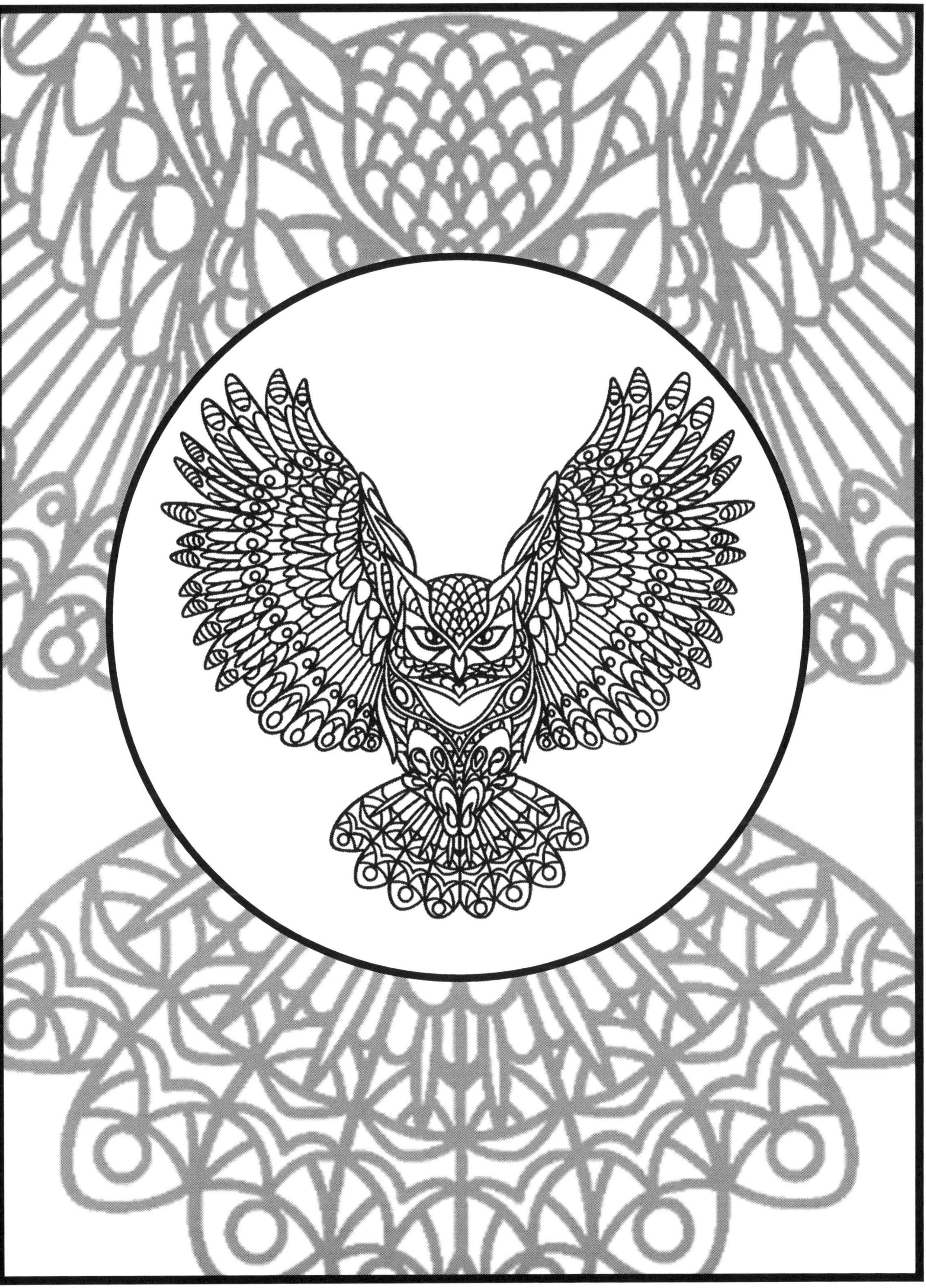

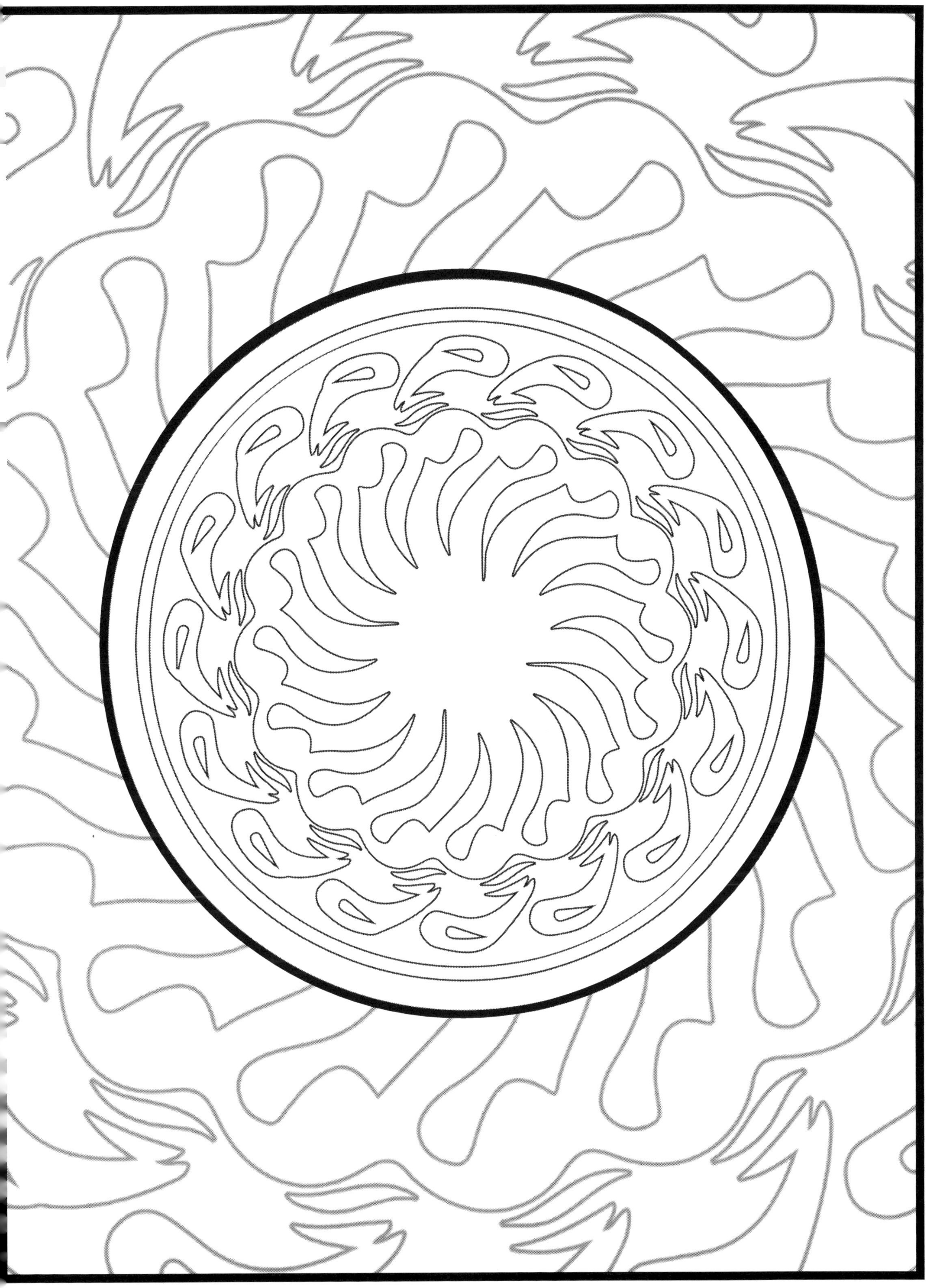

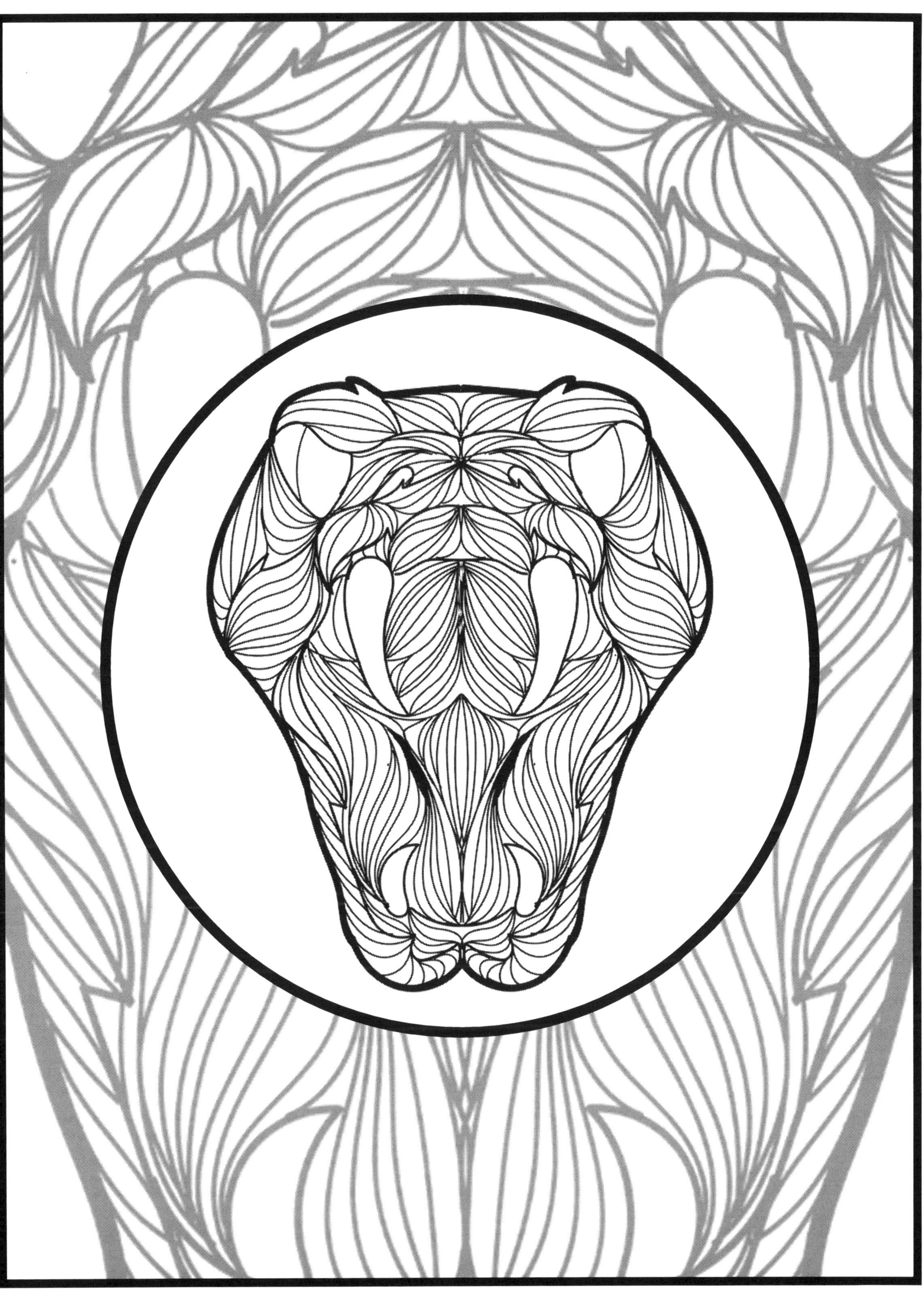

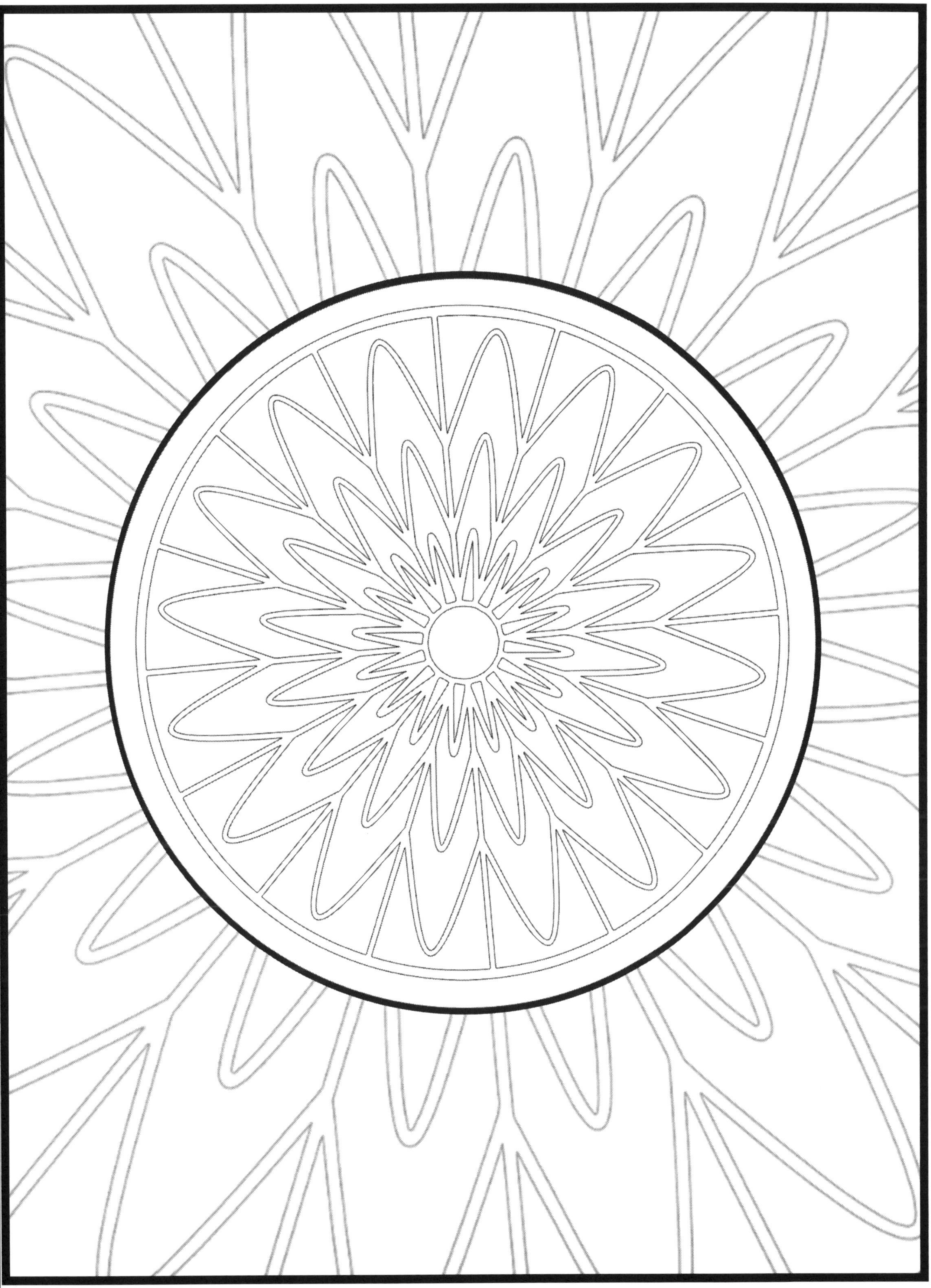

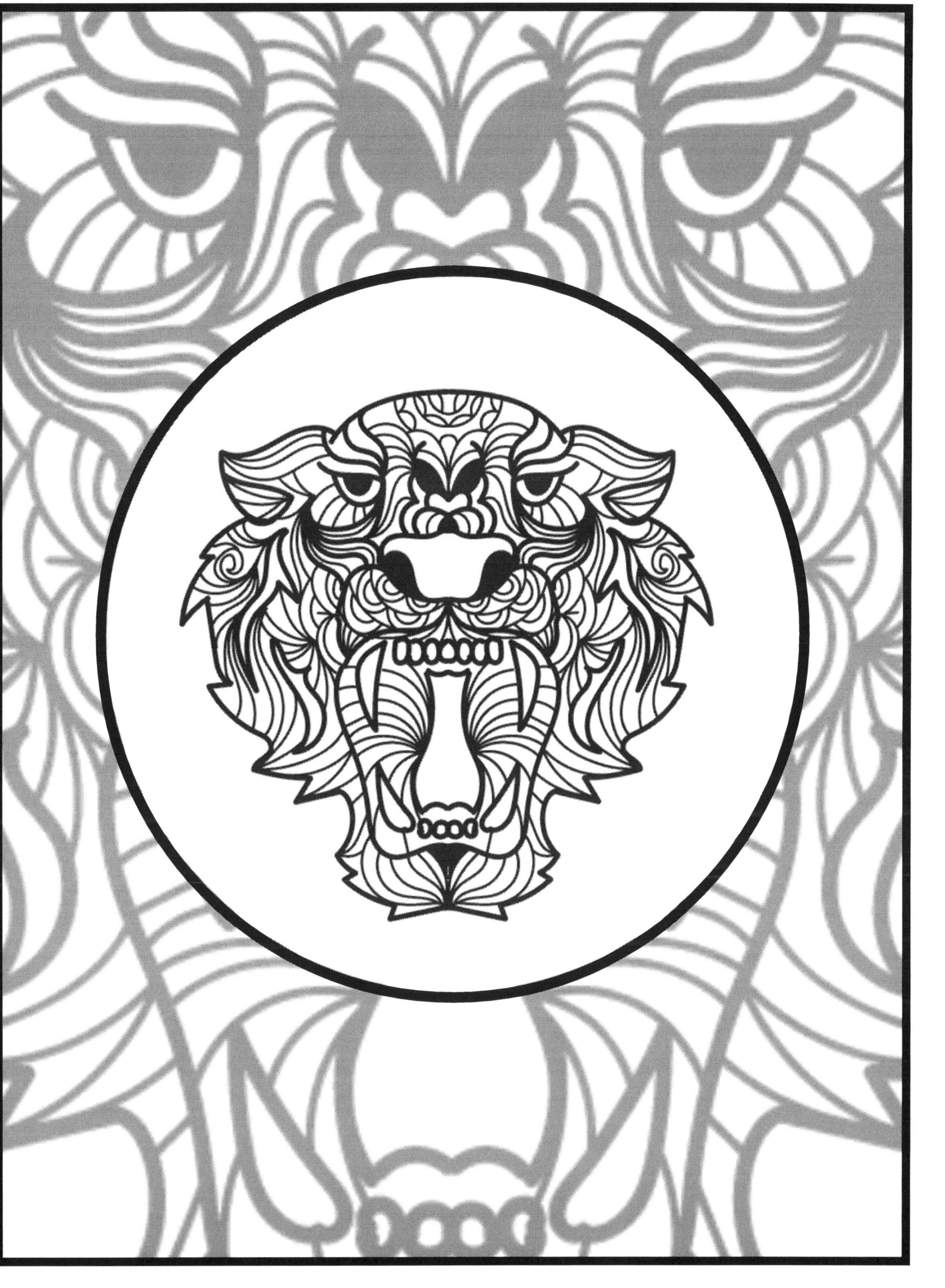

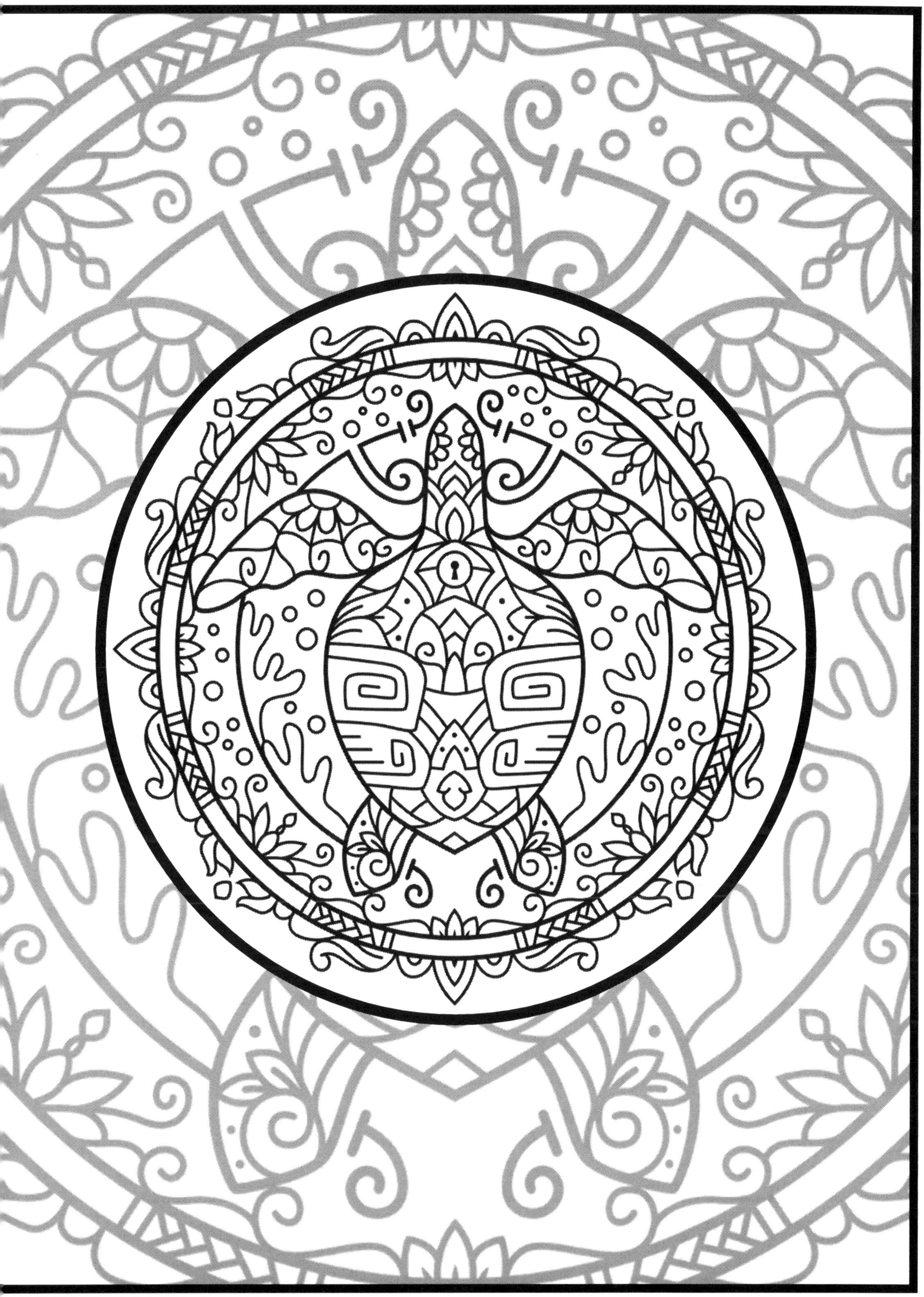

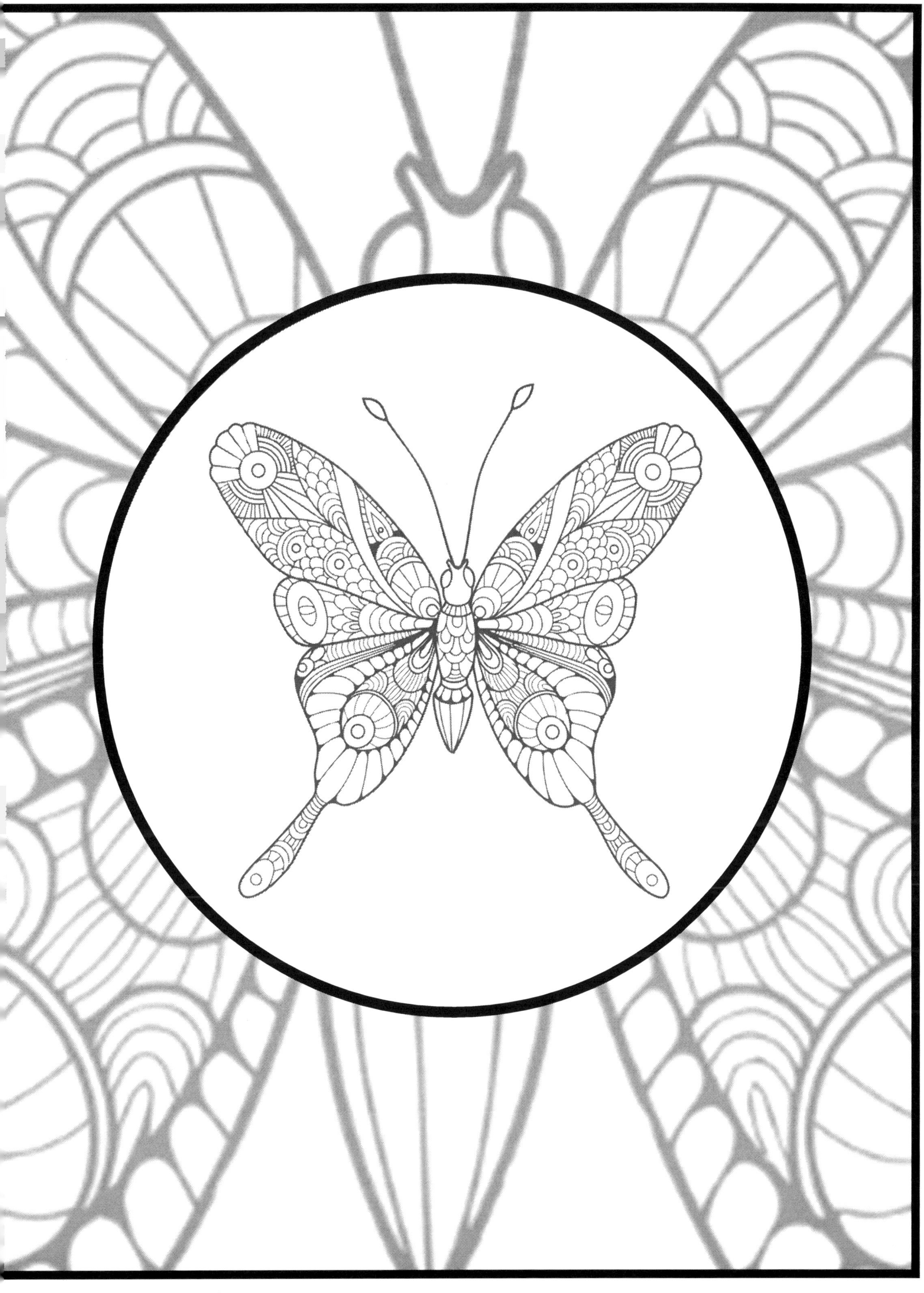

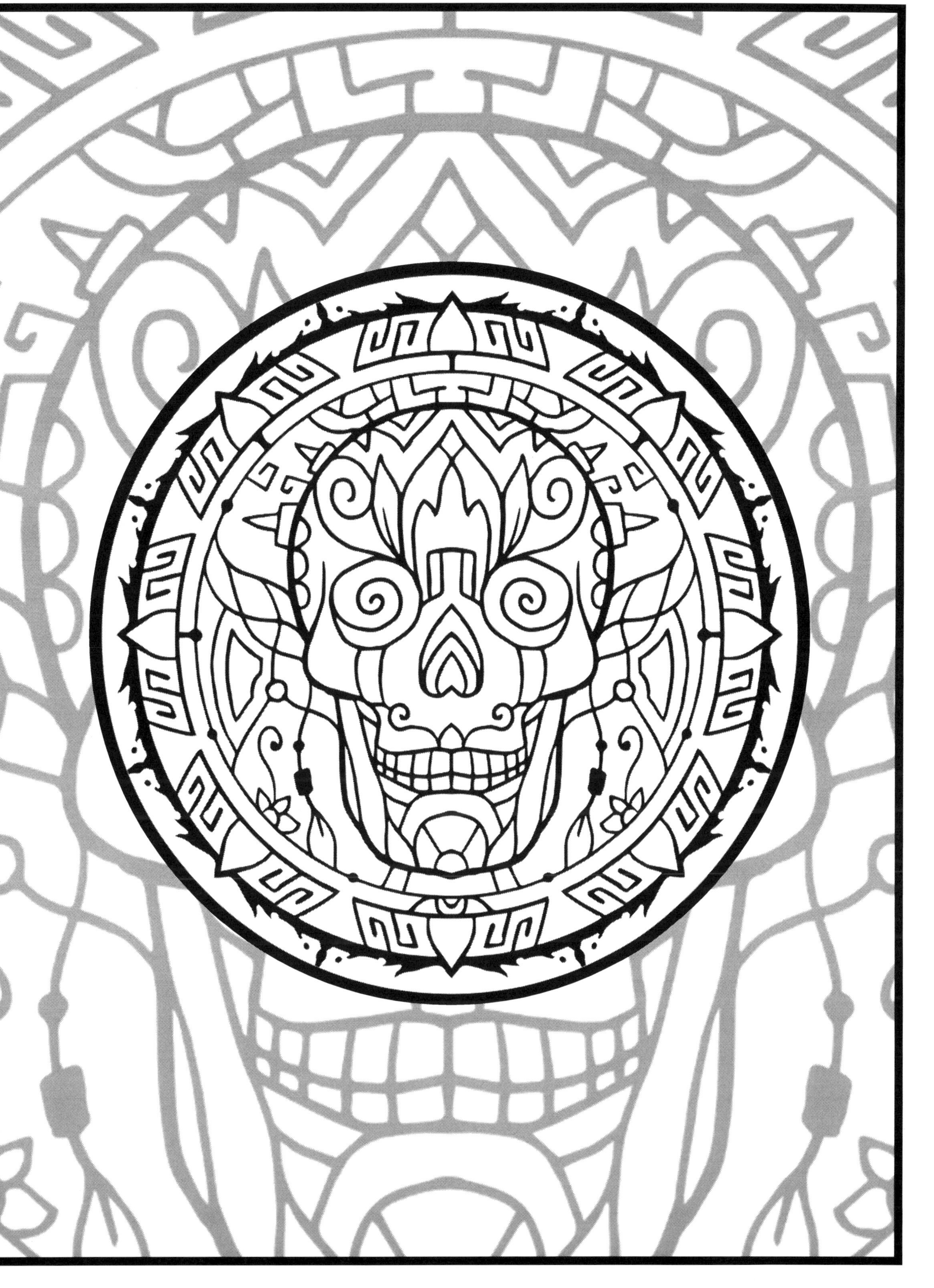

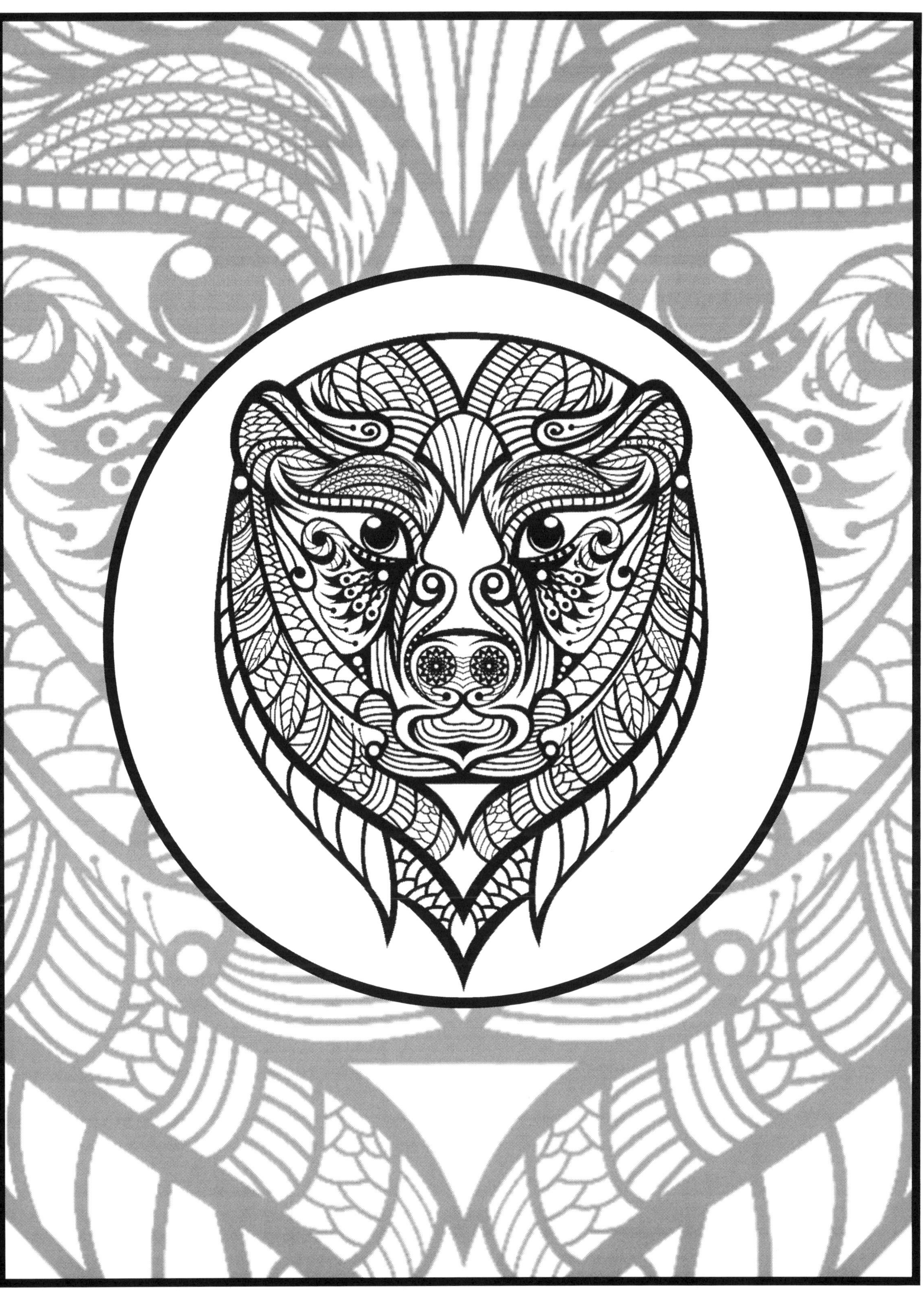

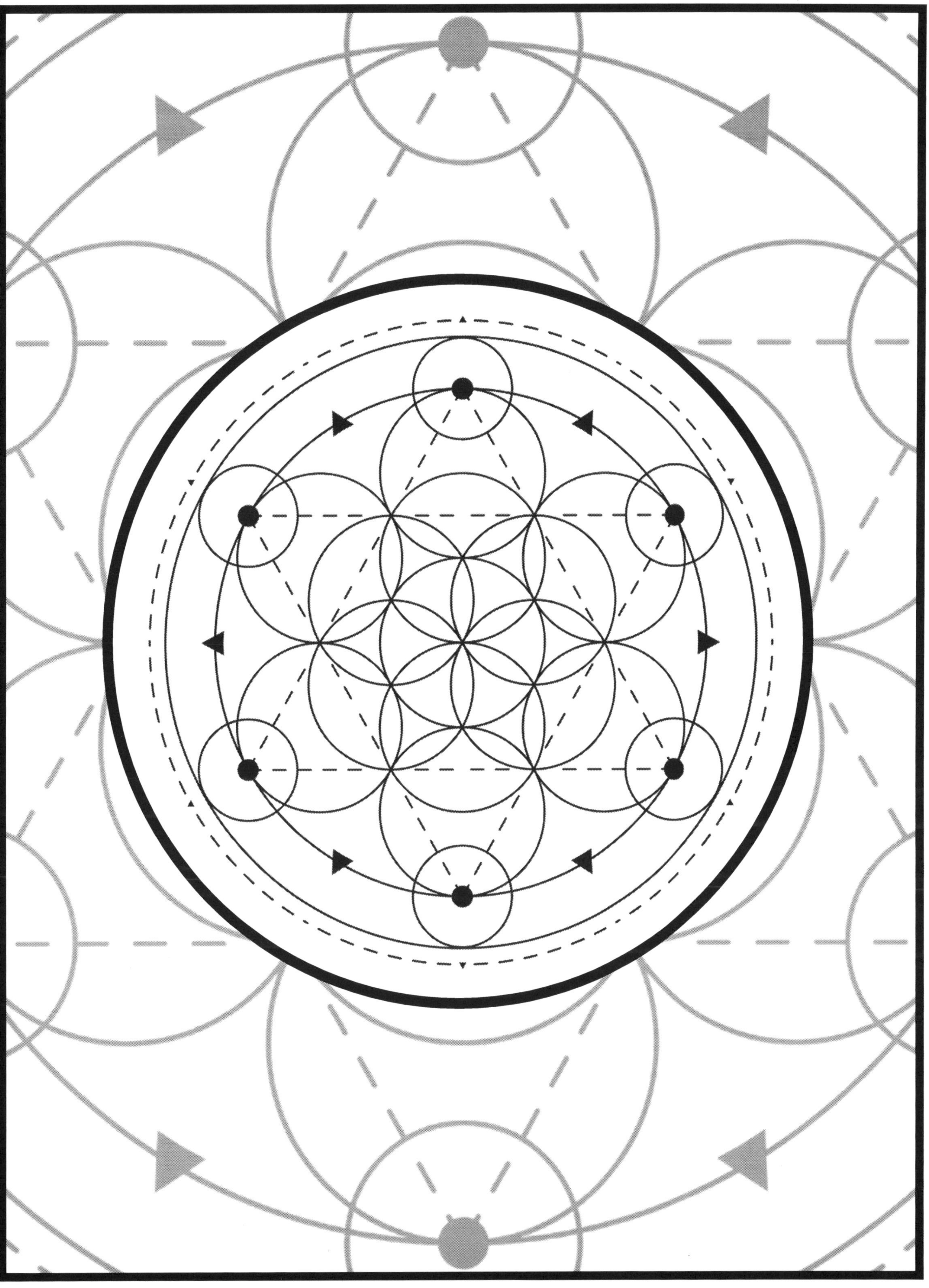

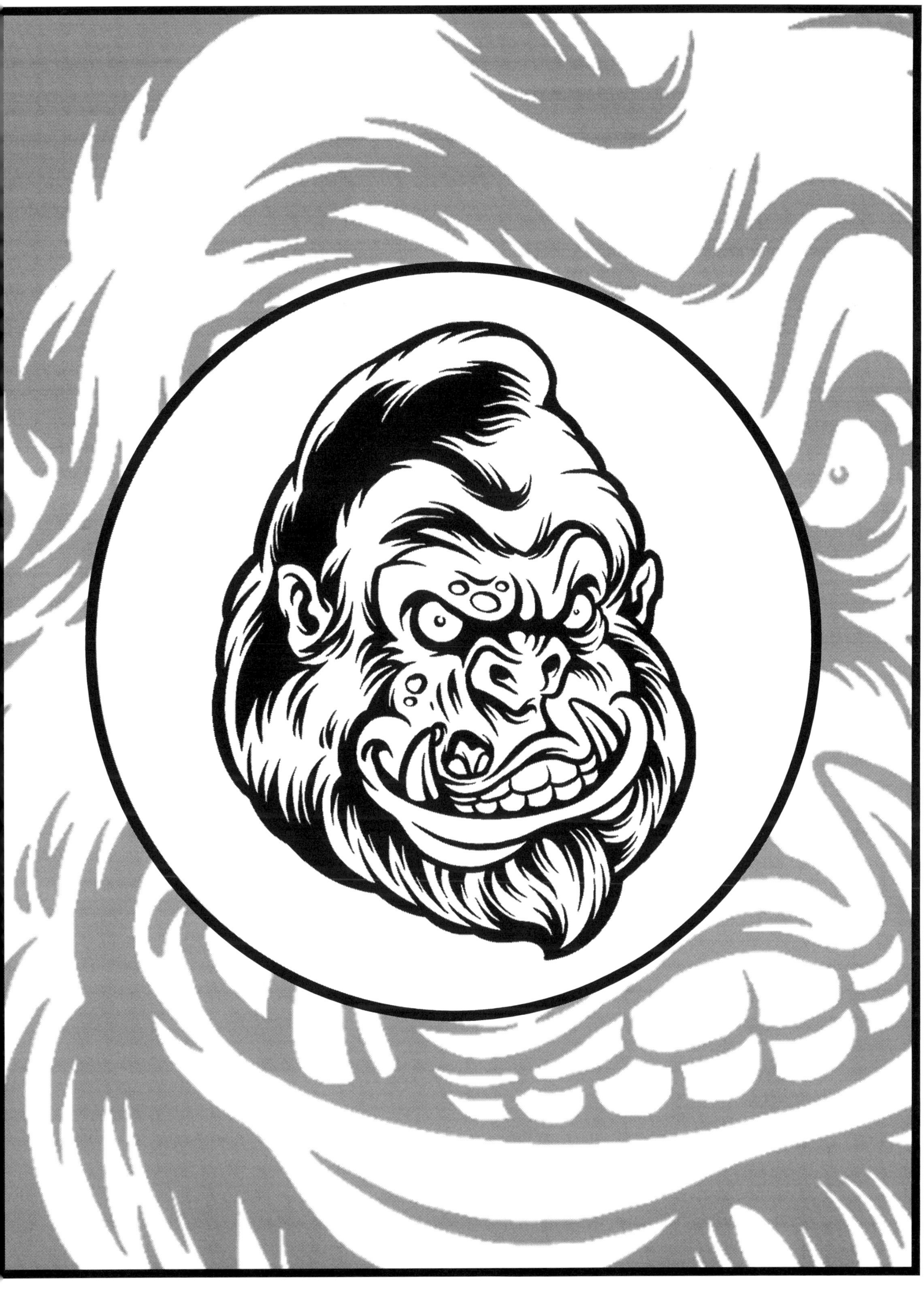

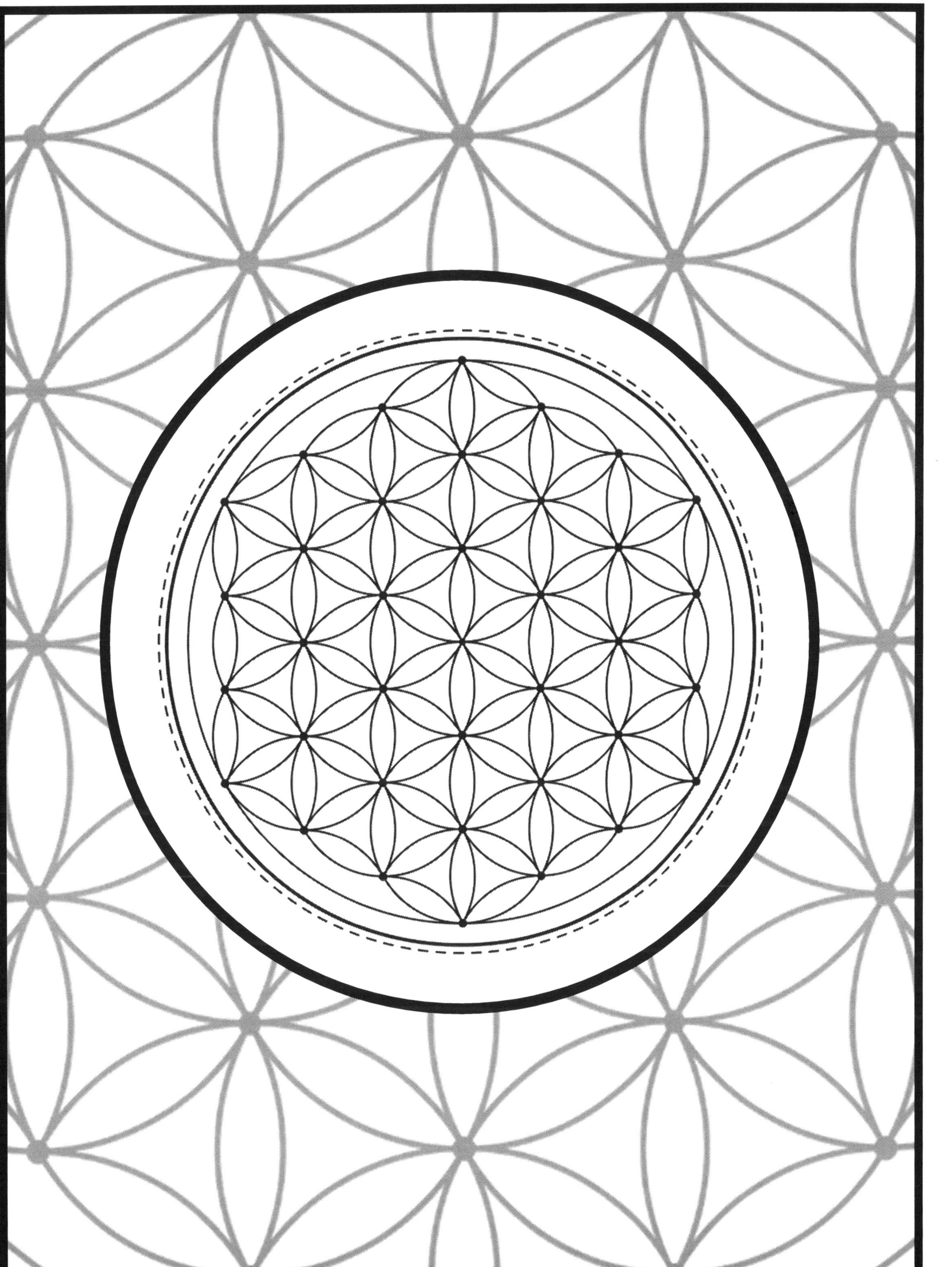

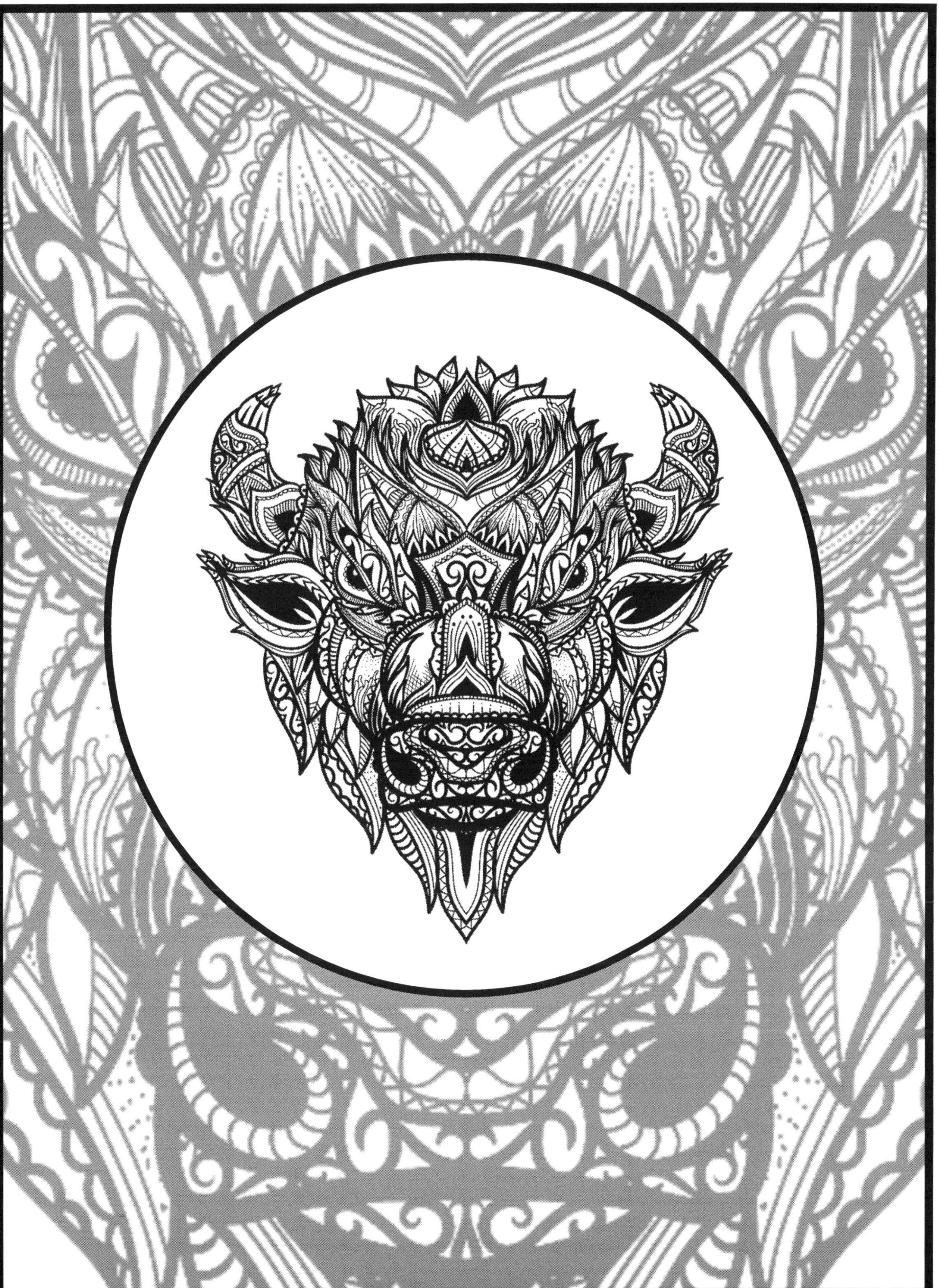

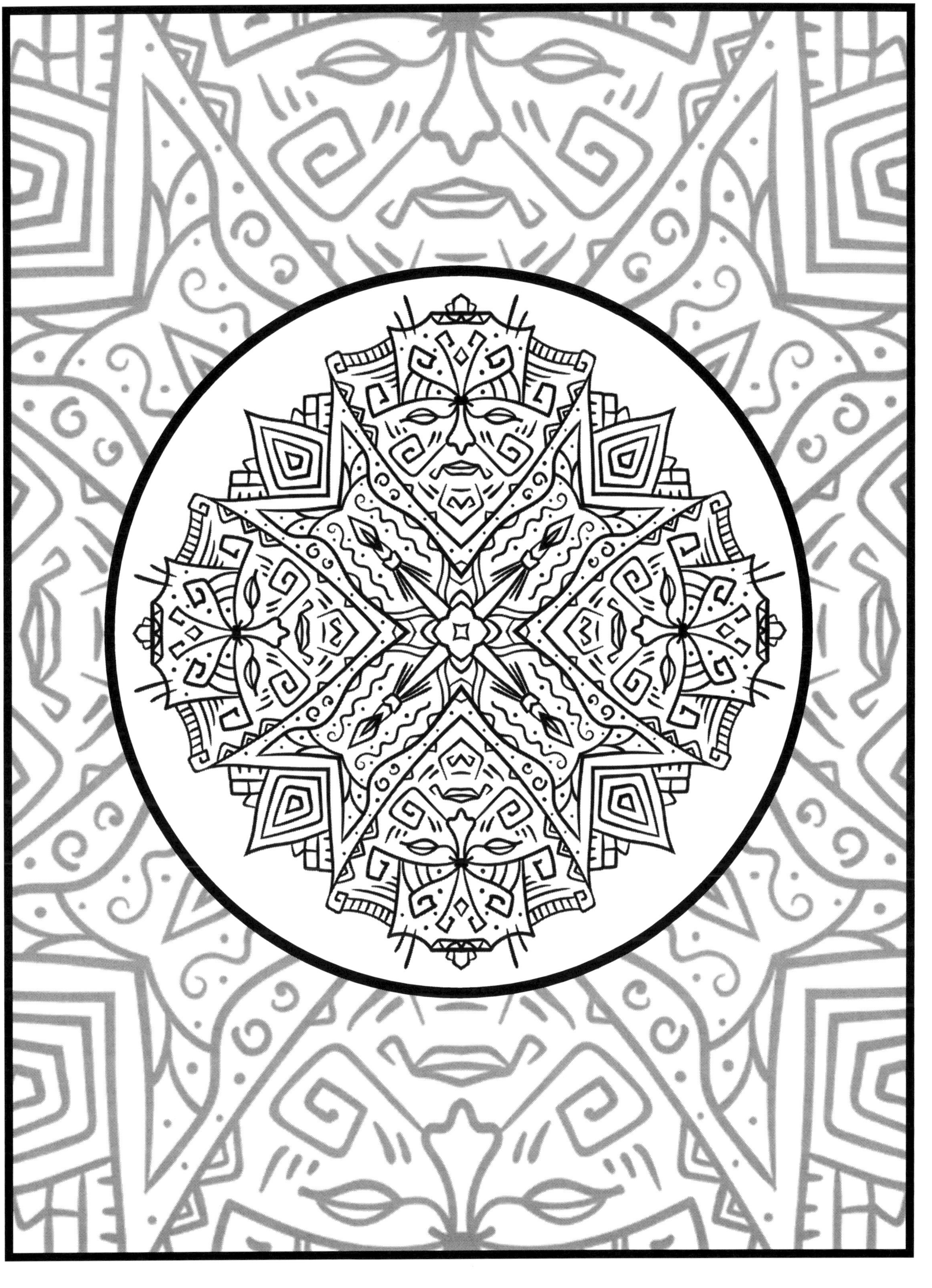

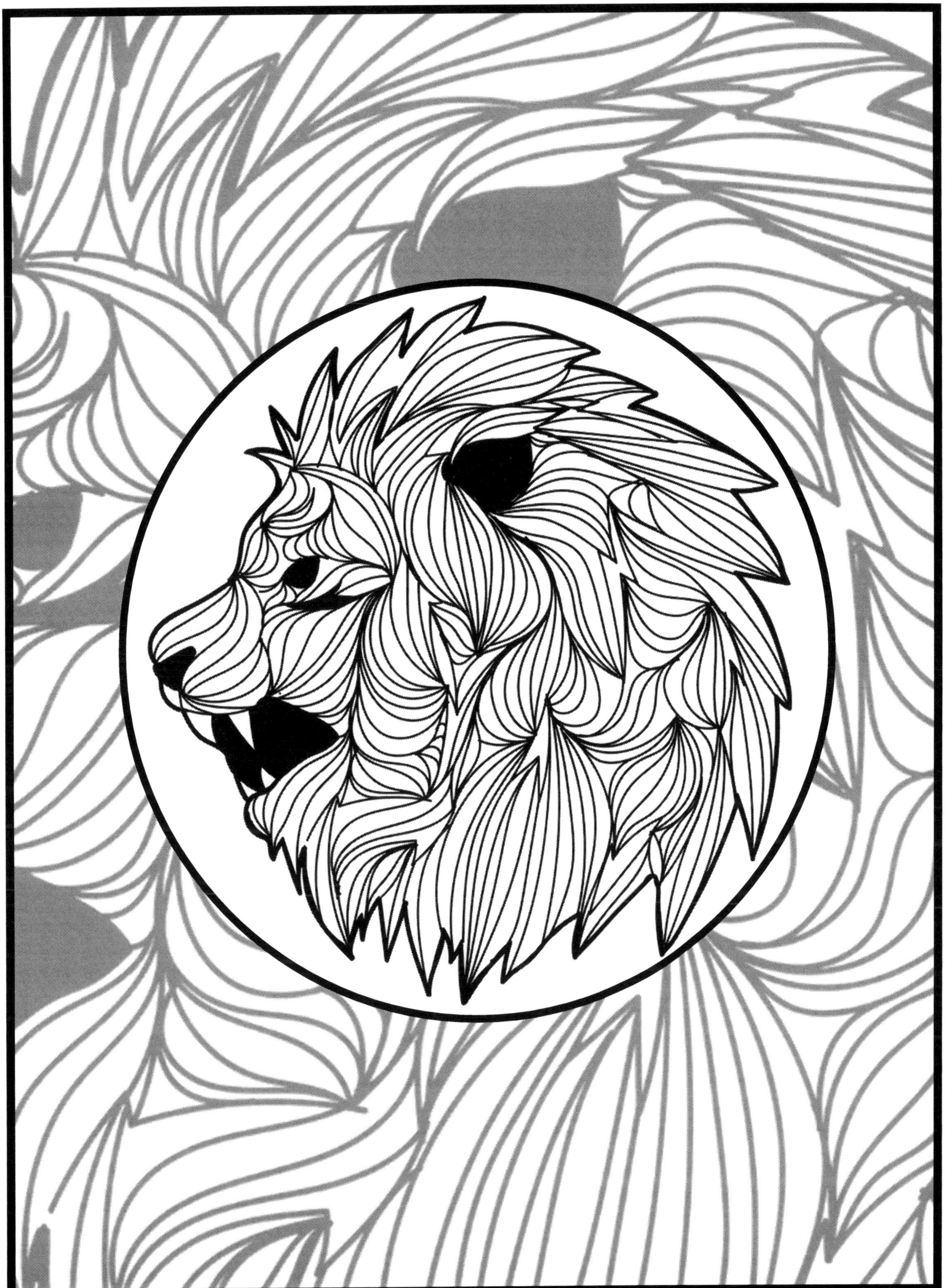

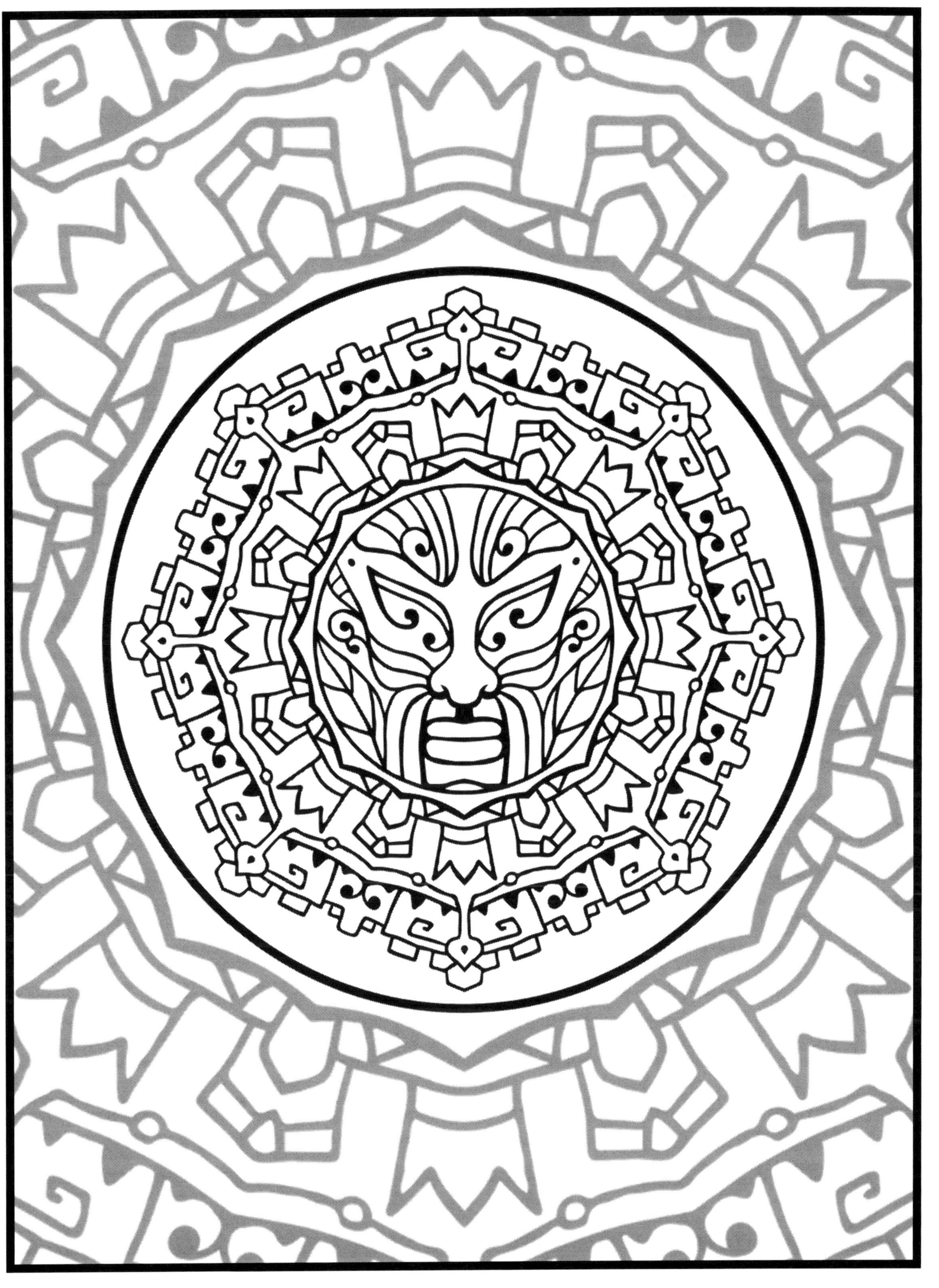

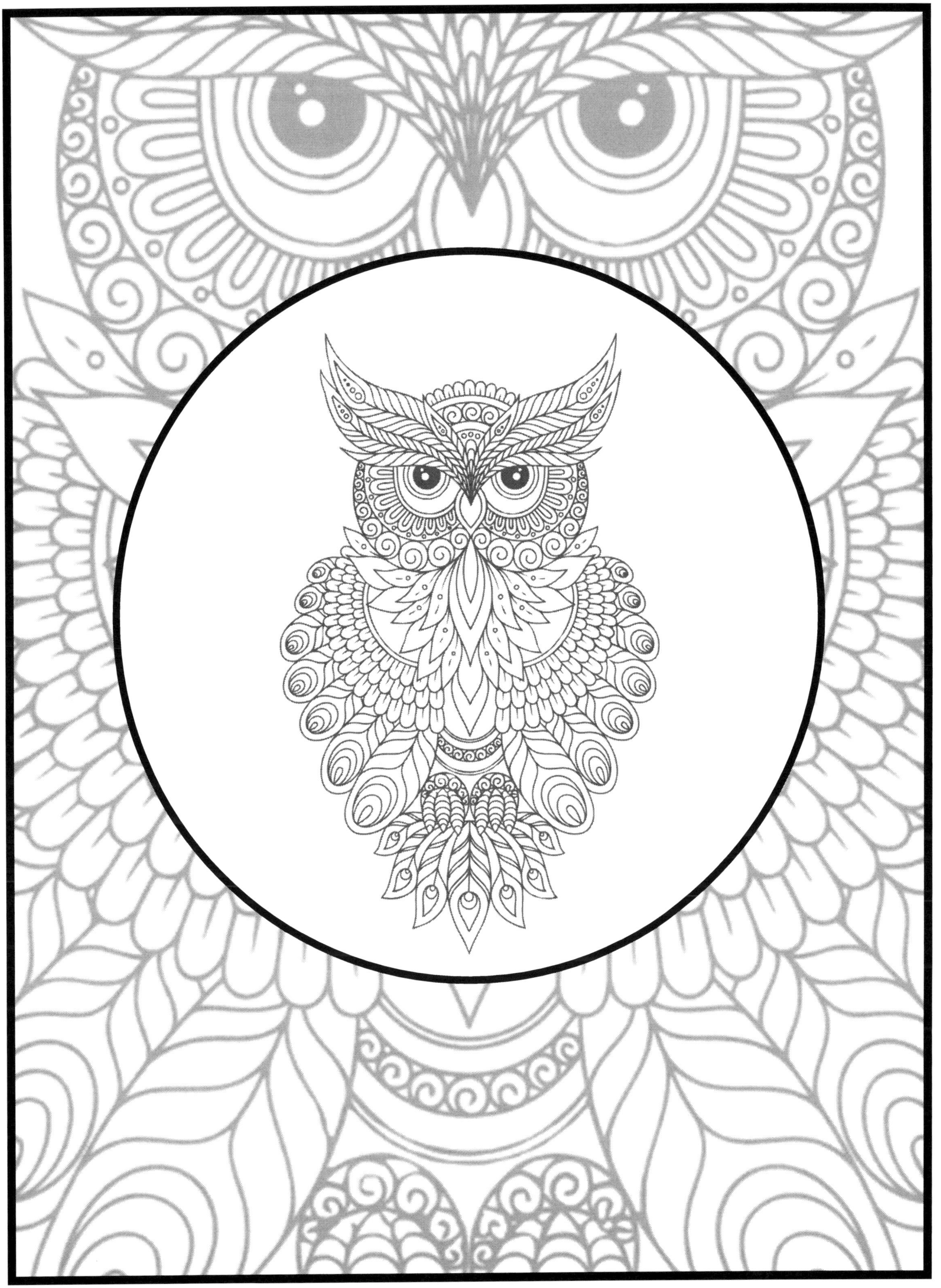

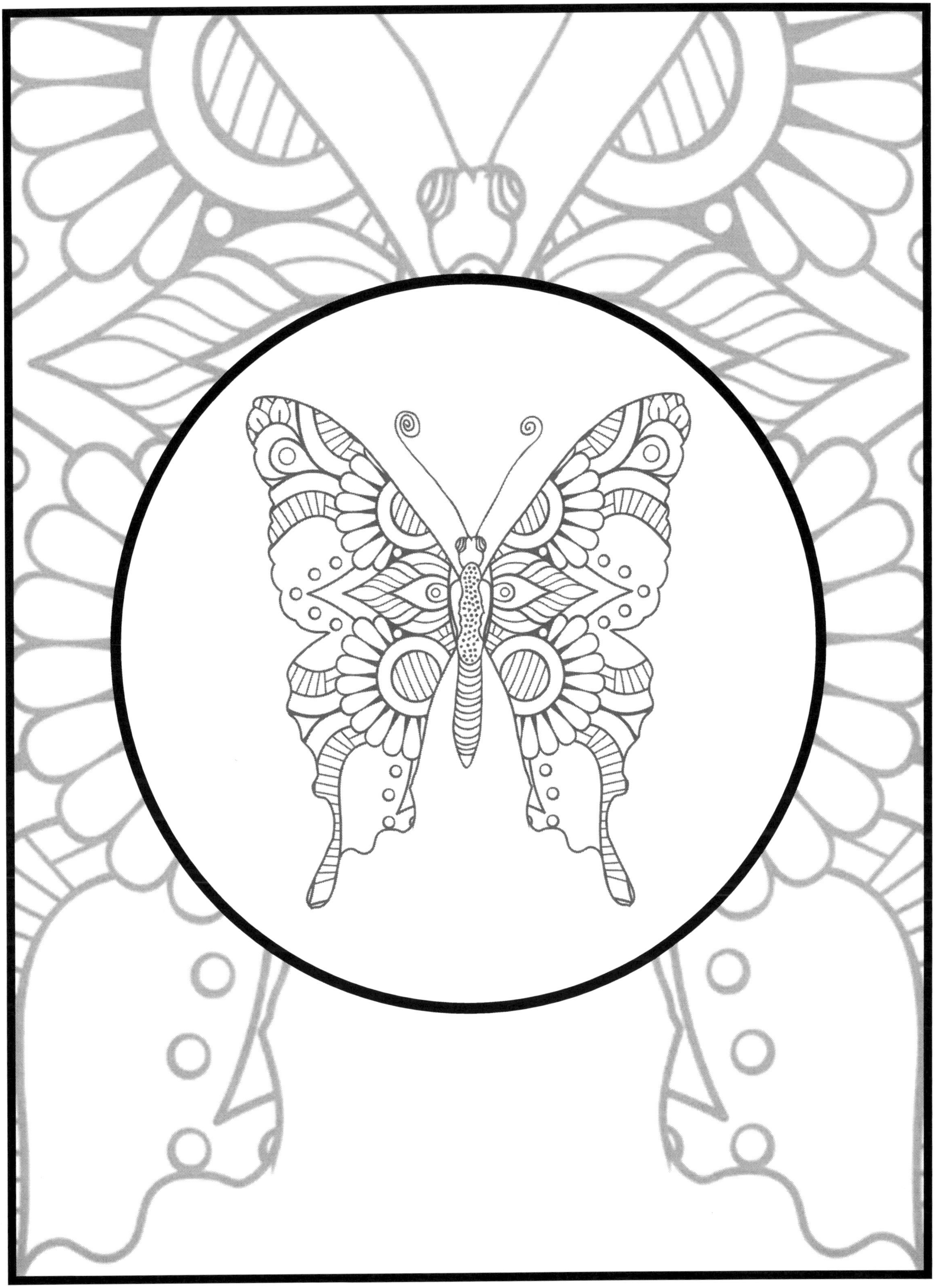

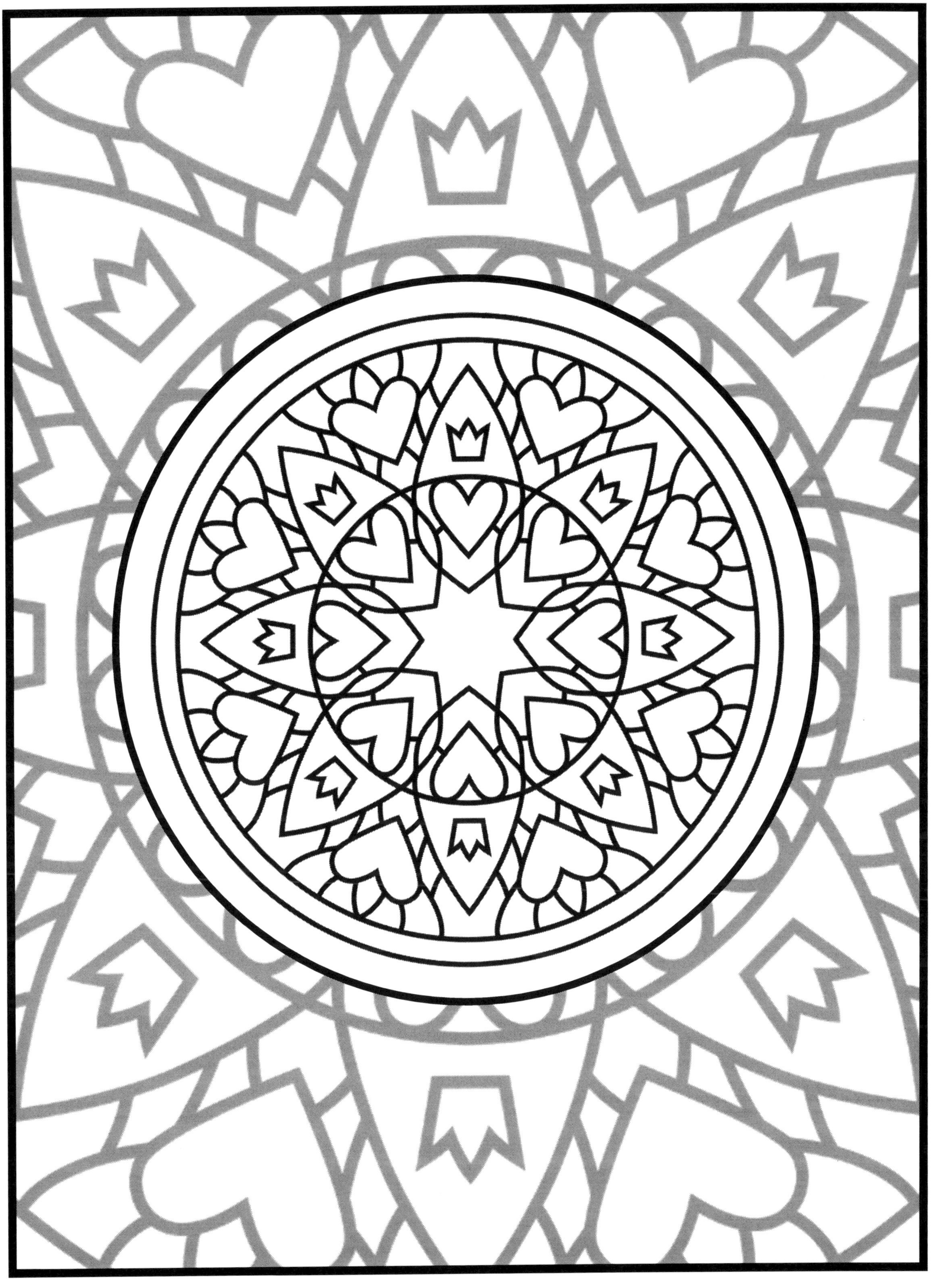

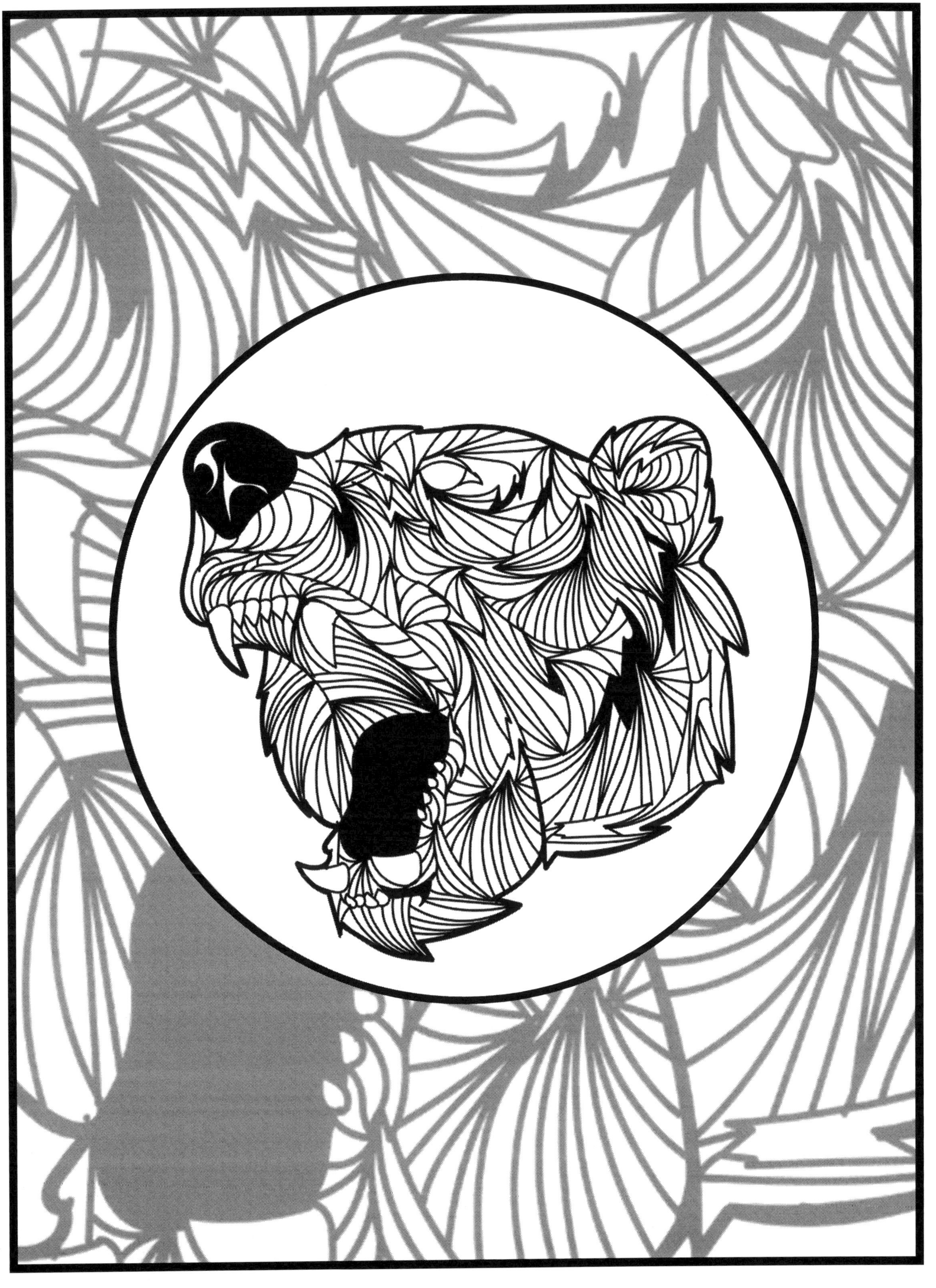

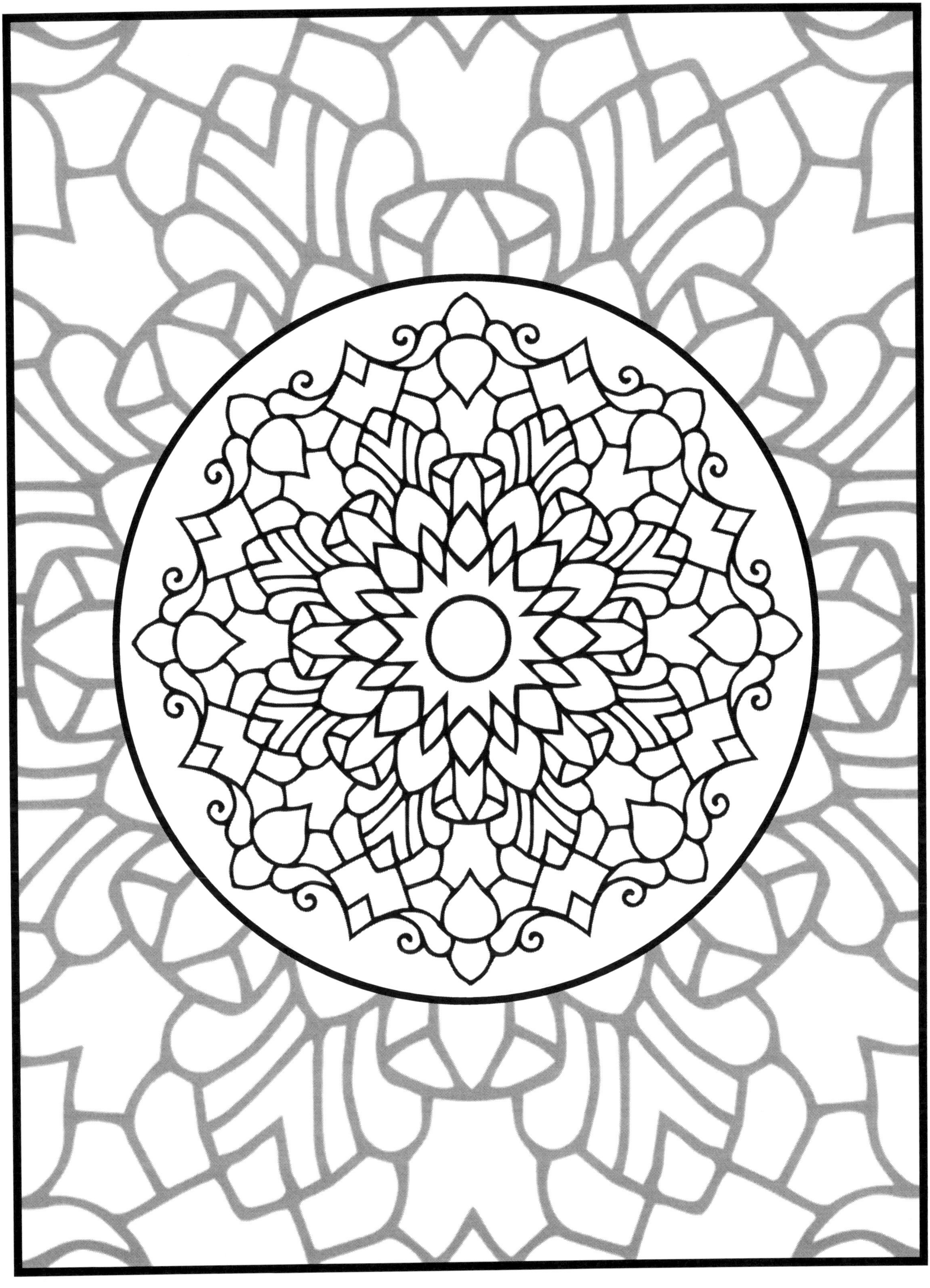

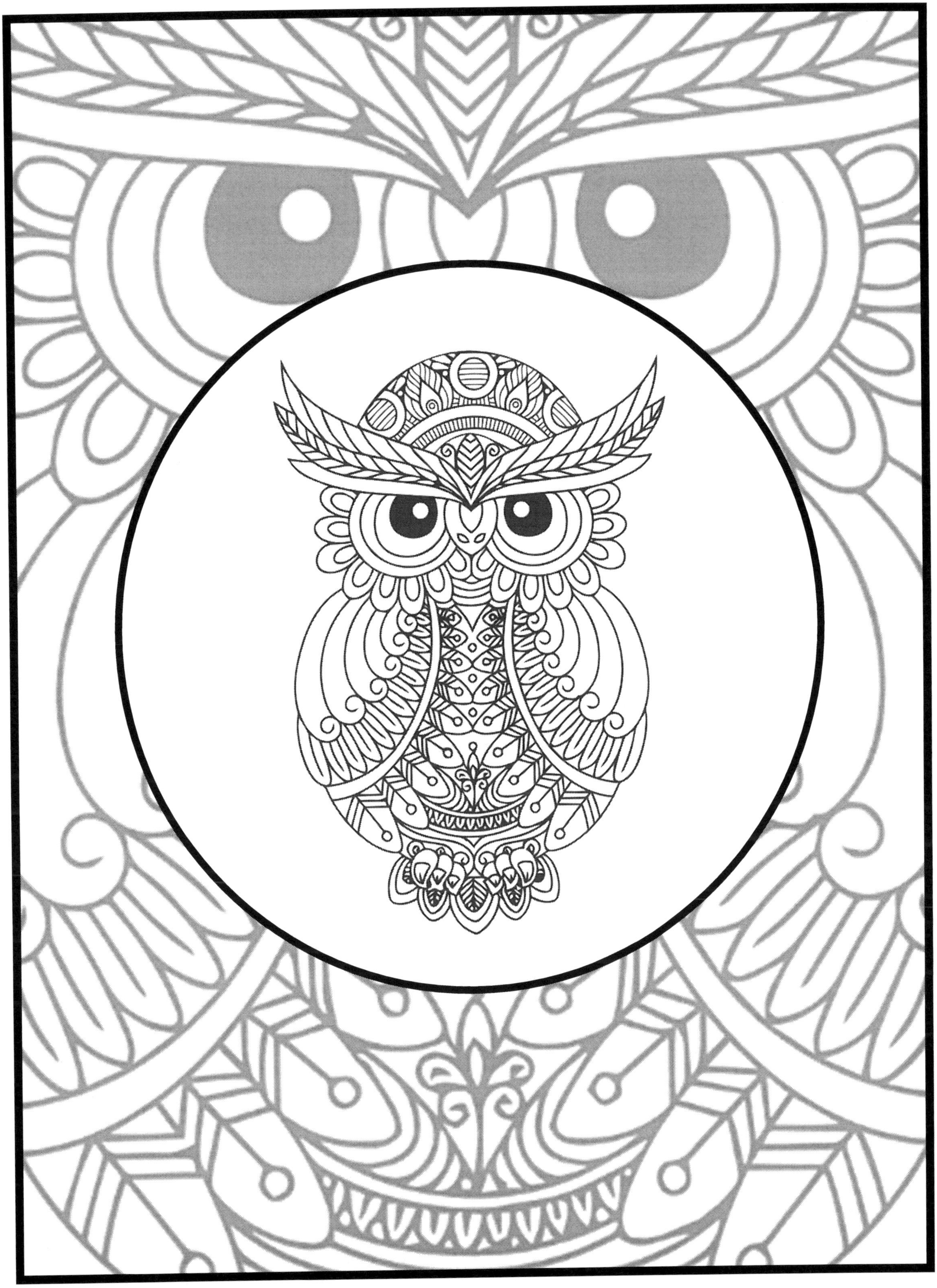

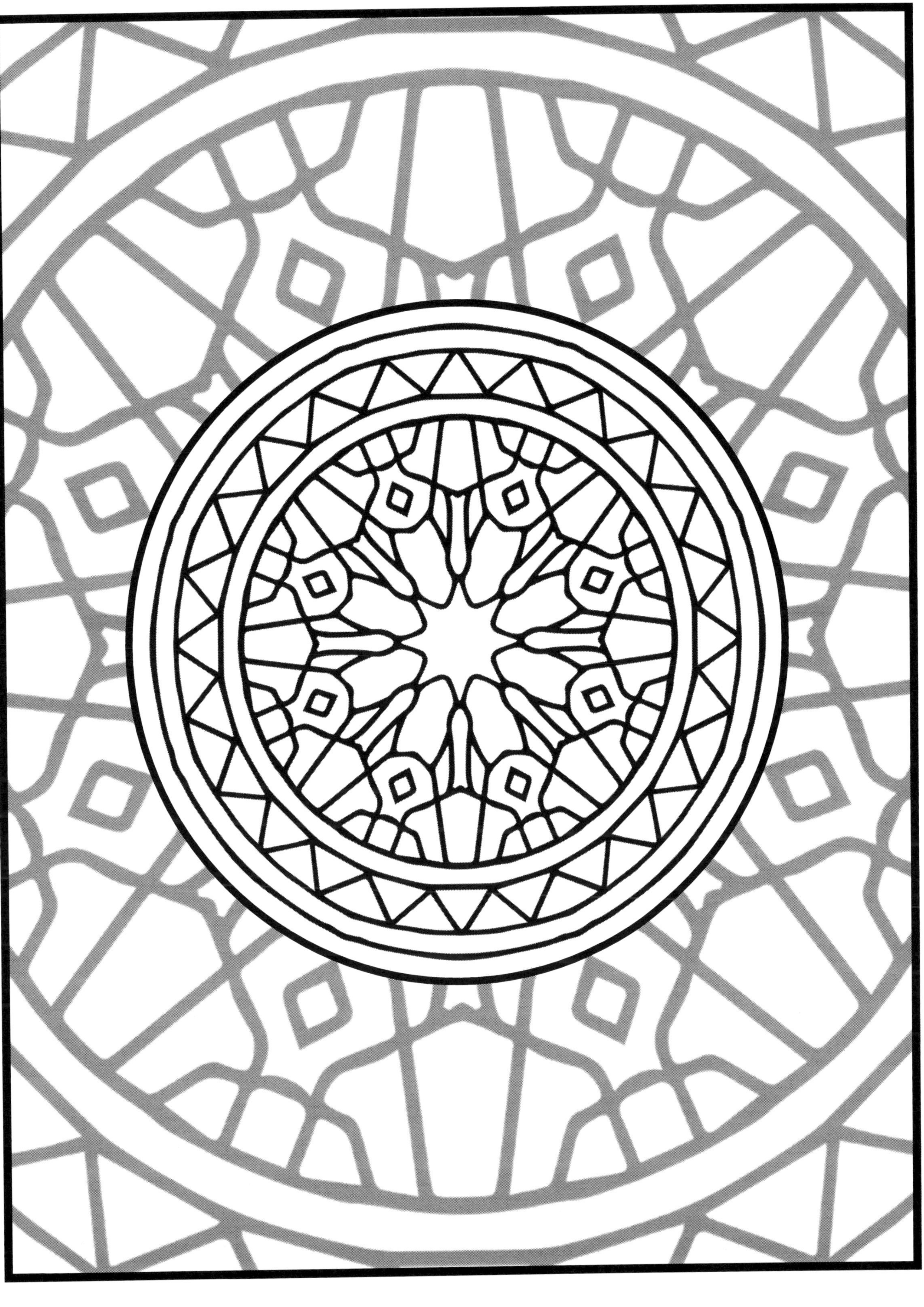

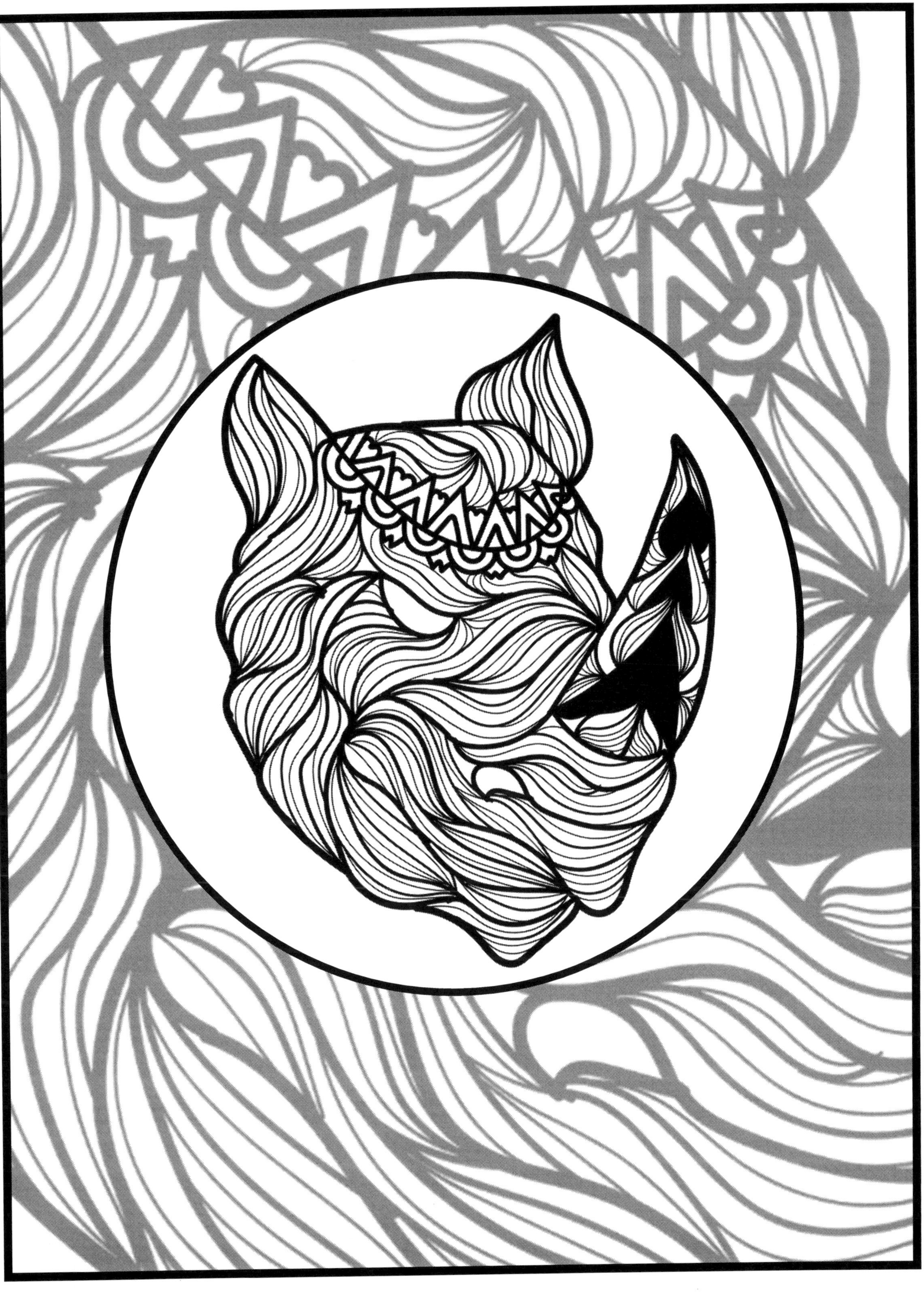

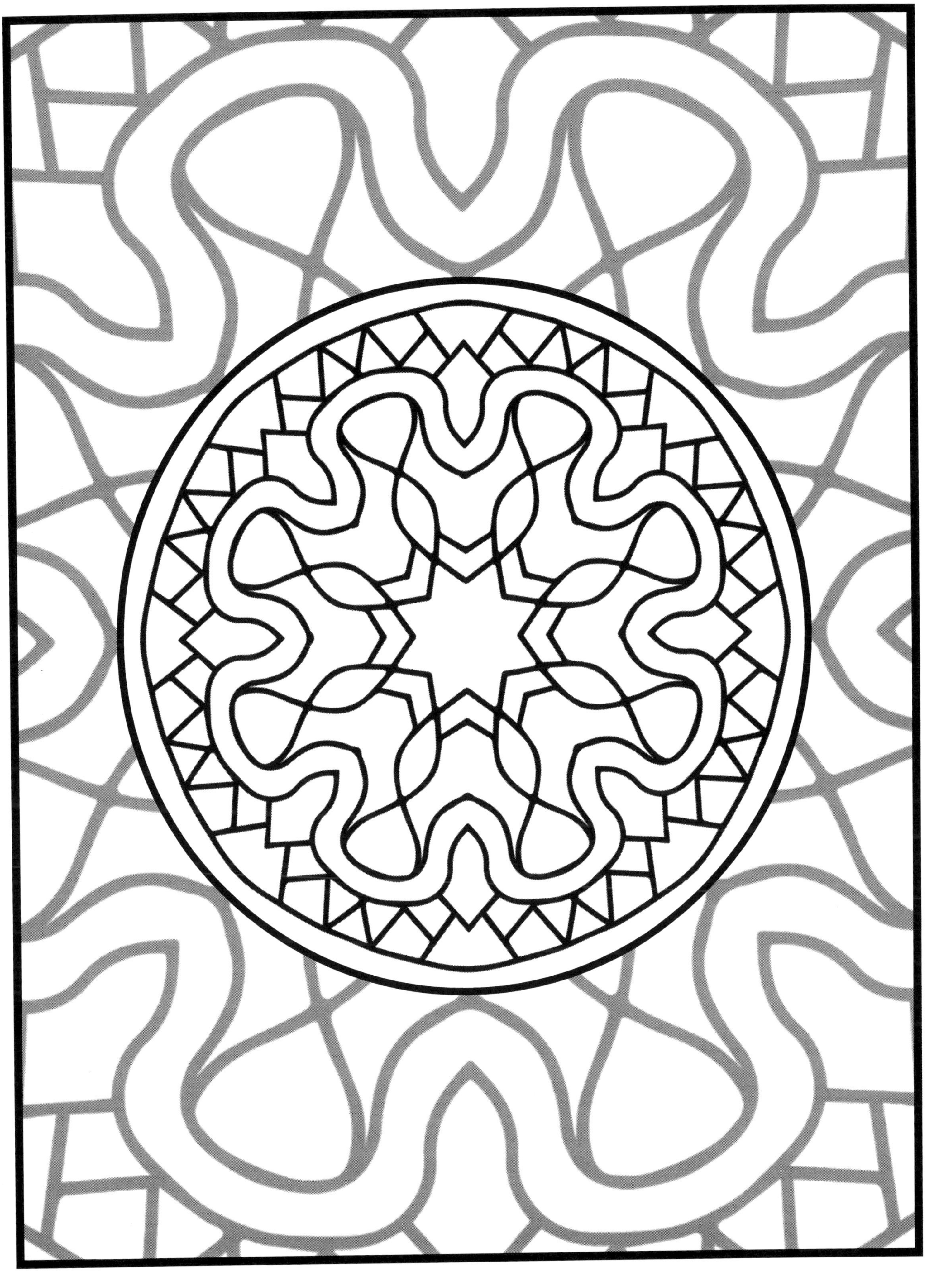

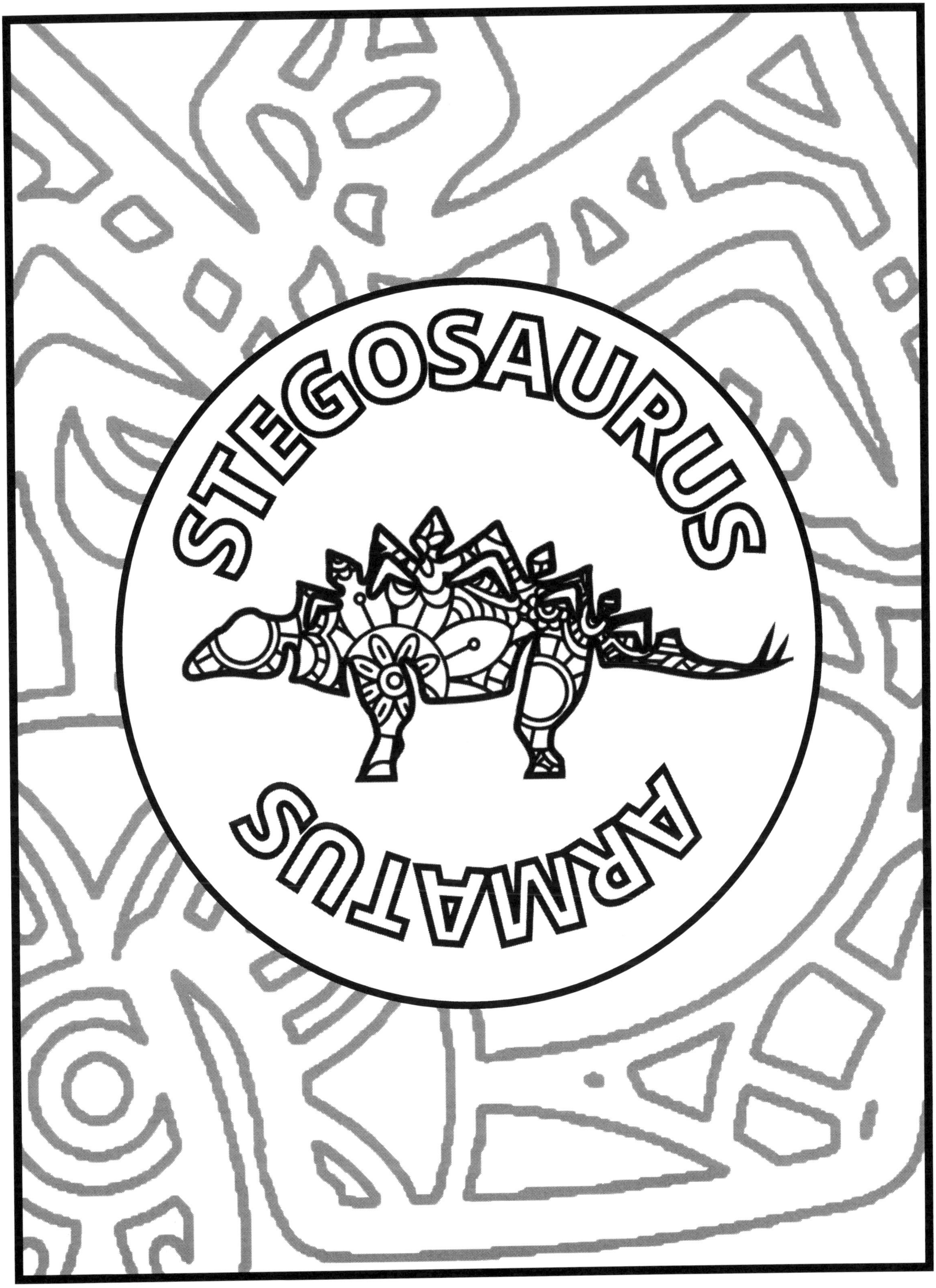
STEGOSAURUS
ARMATUS

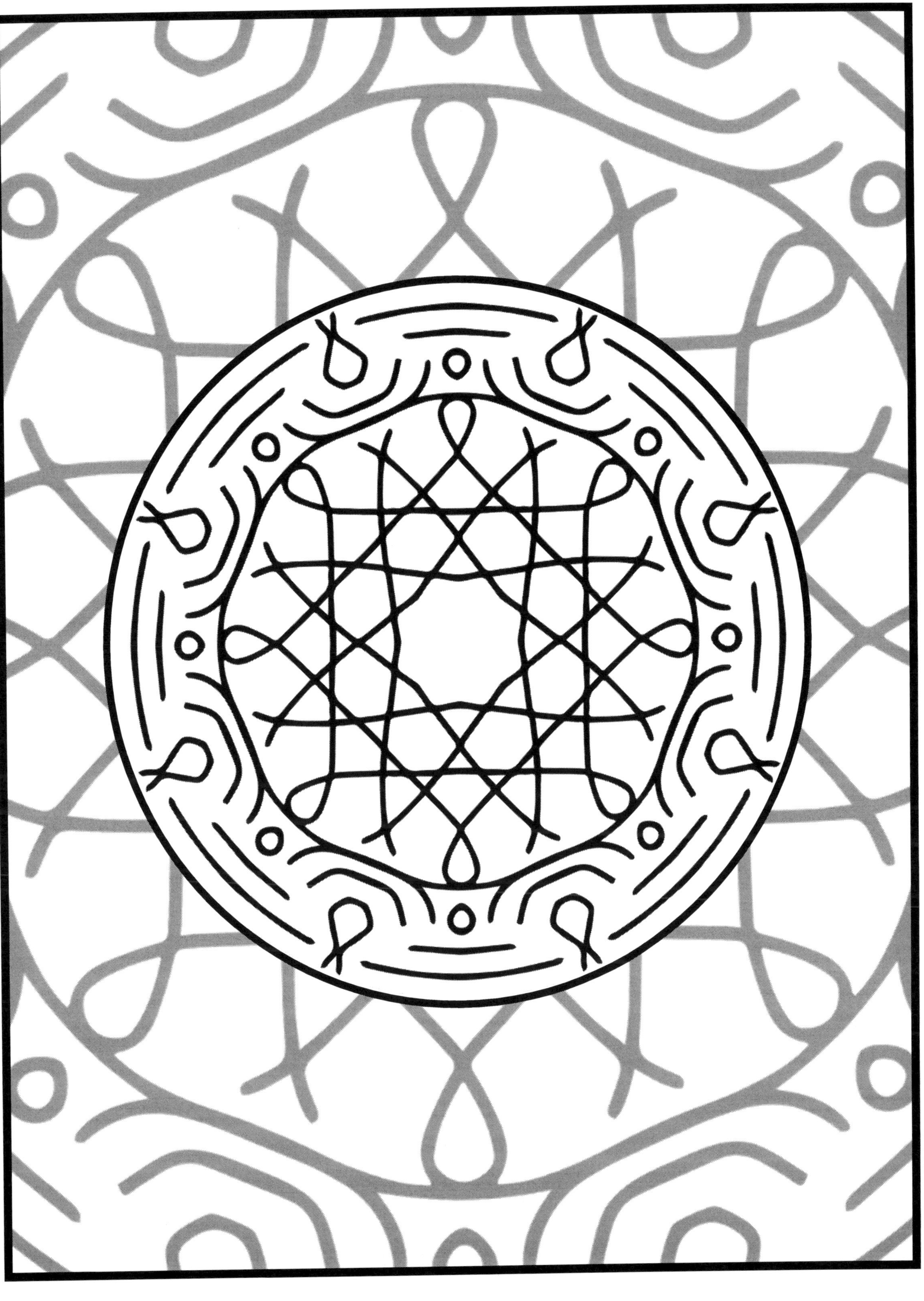

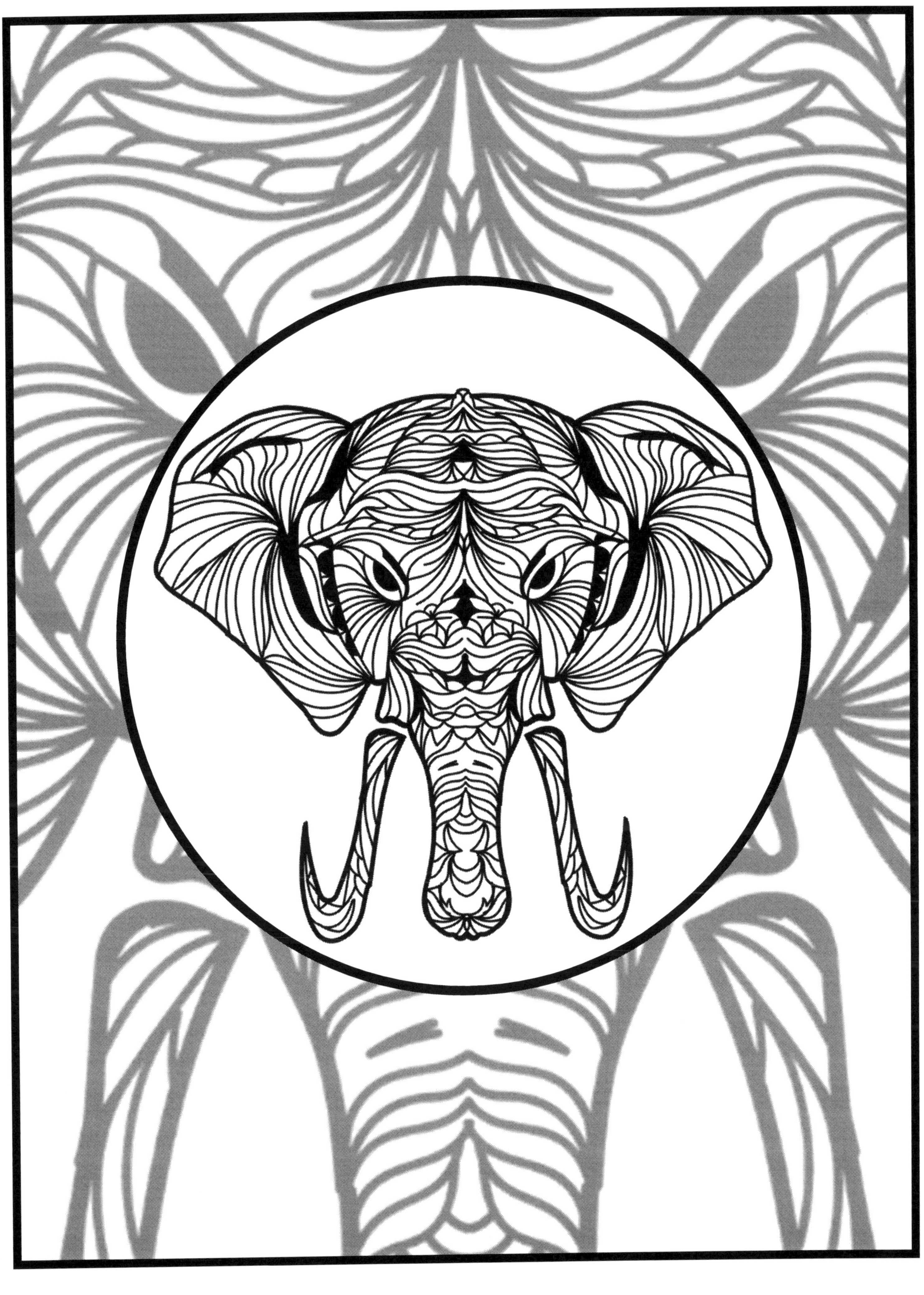

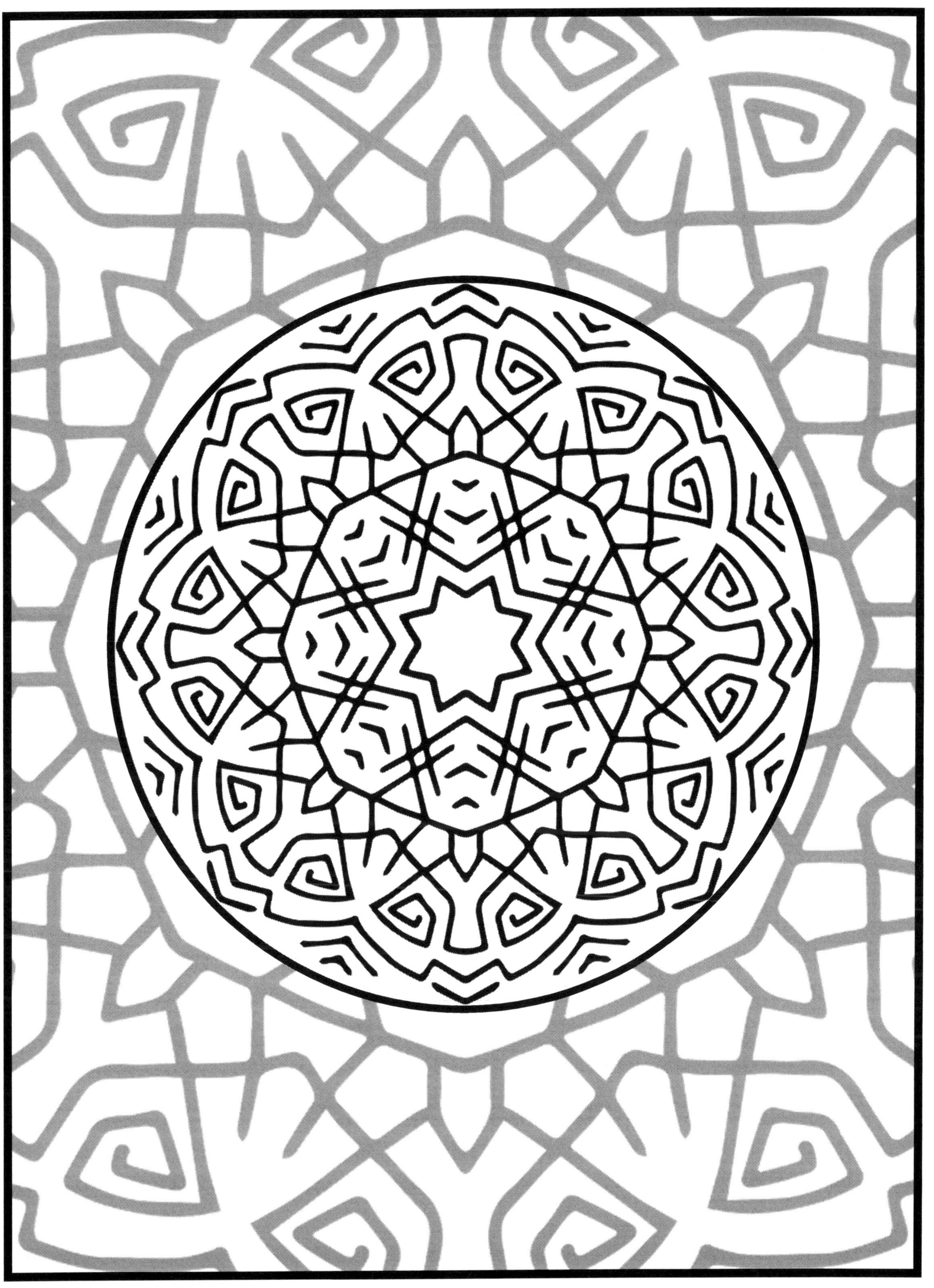

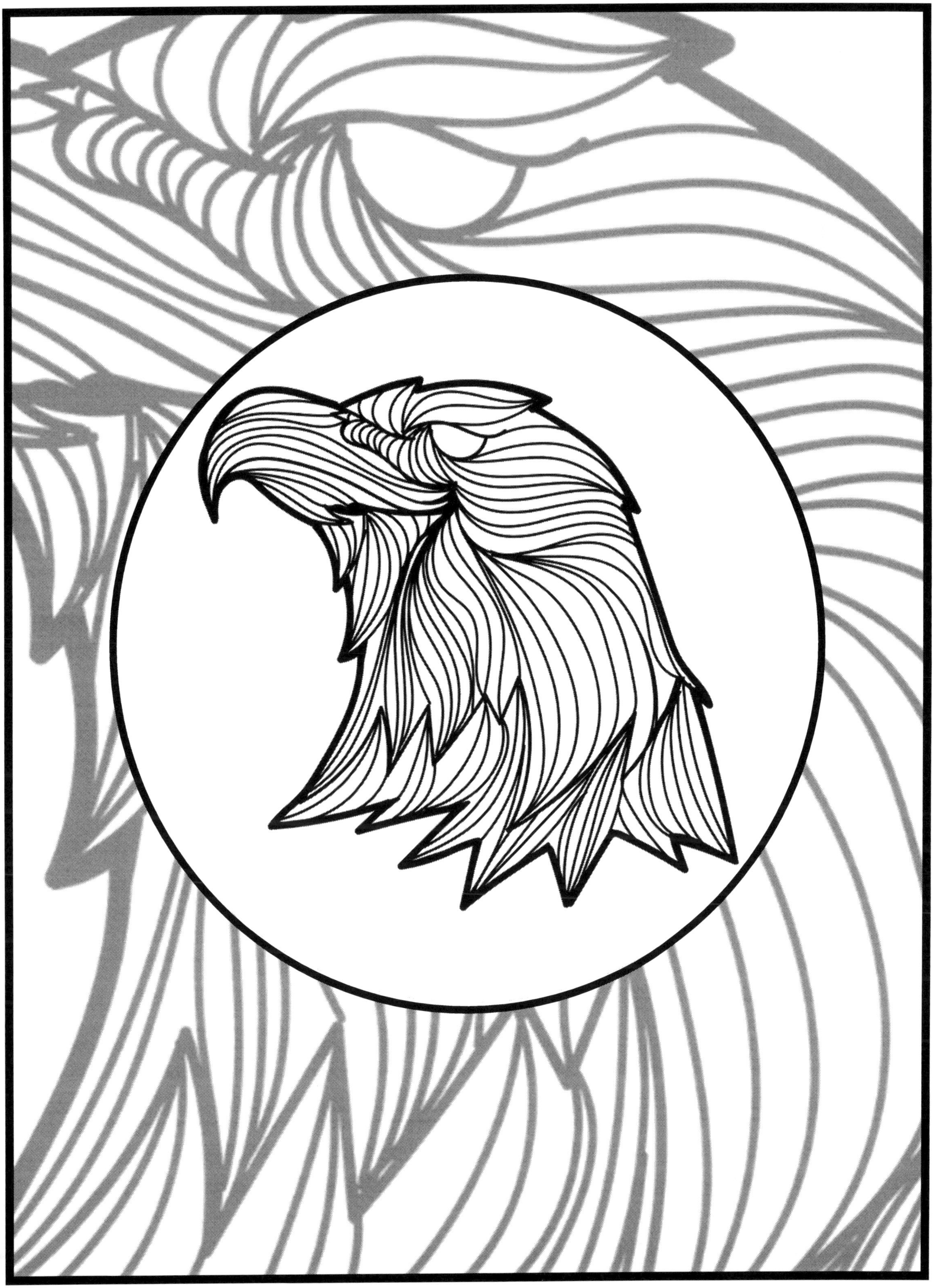

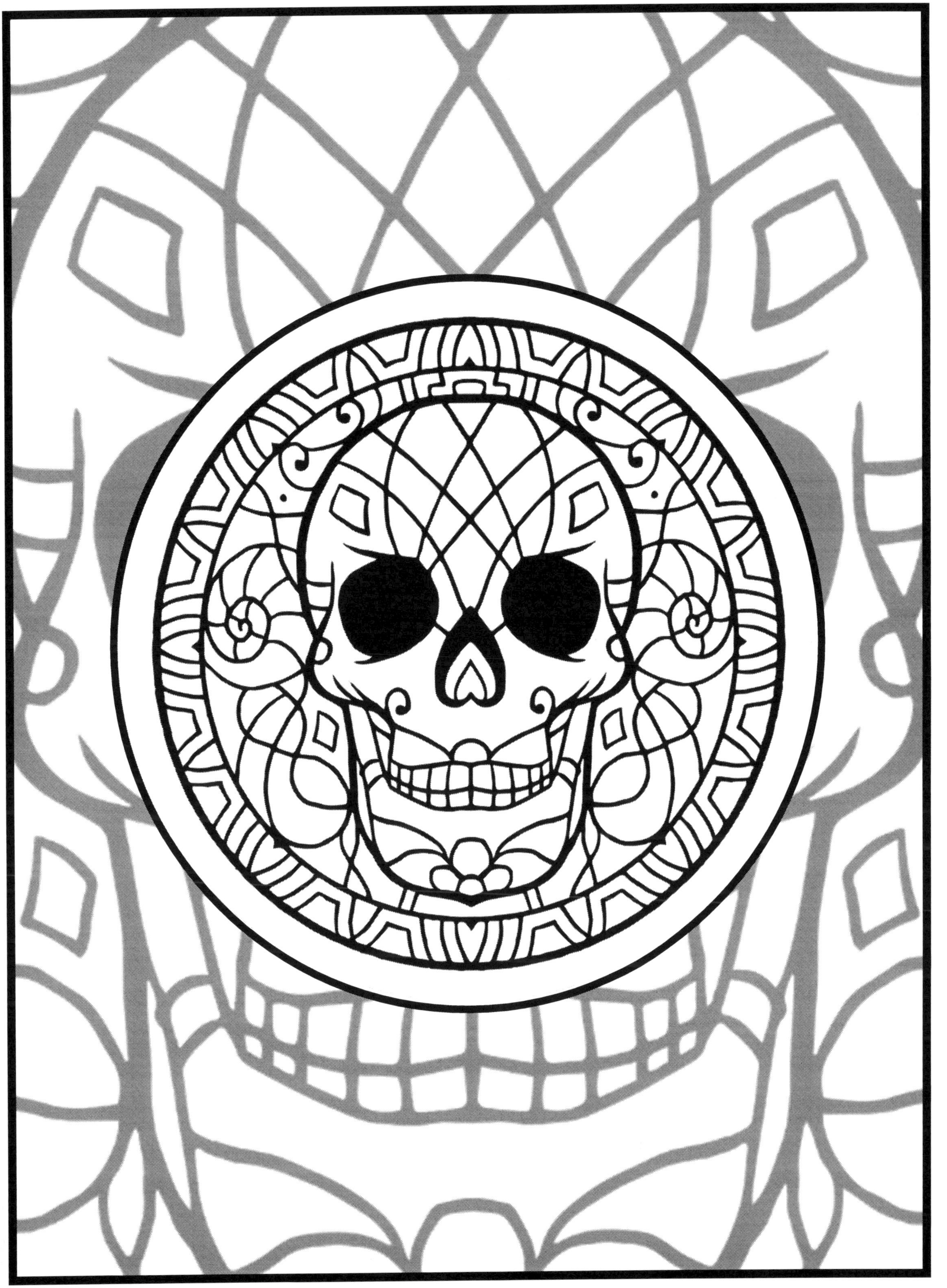

TRUE NORTH OF NORMAL

Manufactured by Amazon.ca
Bolton, ON

24938785R00048